6 $\frac{00}{01}$ мн

HEMISPHERES NORTH AND SOUTH

HEMISPHERES NORTH AND SOUTH

ECONOMIC DISPARITY
AMONG NATIONS

BY

DAVID HOROWITZ

THE JOHNS HOPKINS PRESS
BALTIMORE

PREFACE

The second industrial revolution, the atomic age and its technological transformation, the population explosion and the end of colonialism, the awakening of Asia and Africa and the independence of their new nations, the rise of China, with its power and peril, all press hard on our century. Their concomitants in the social and economic fields are the emergence of a managed economy and of the welfare state and the economic problems of the underdeveloped nations.

With modern technology, space and natural resources are slowly and gradually receding in importance as the main economic determinants of the standards of society, while capital, skill, and know-how assume greater weight and influence. The successful application of anticyclical policies, the birth of the welfare state, the progress of economic growth combined with full employment and relative stability, the narrowing of gulfs between social classes by a deliberate redistribution of national income—these socioeconomic processes have injected a fresh and non-Utopian element of humanism into economic policy and practice.

There could hardly be a more fitting subject for the kind of conscious guidance of economic processes reflected in the welfare state than the economic conditions of underdeveloped peoples. In a speech on foreign aid on March 22, 1961, the late President Kennedy made the following statement:

> The economic collapse of those free but less-developed nations which now stand poised between sustained growth and economic chaos would be disastrous to our national security, harmful to our comparative prosperity and offensive to our conscience.

40471

v

There exists, in the 1960's, a historic opportunity for a major economic assistance effort by the free industrialized nations to move more than half the people of the less-developed nations into self-sustained economic growth, while the rest move substantially closer to the day when they, too, will no longer have to depend on outside assistance.[1]

The President's comments reflect his awareness, on the one hand, of the shocking economic situation existing among the underdeveloped nations, with all the dangers inherent in that situation, and, on the other, of the possibility of changing it.

The attempt to arrive at a synthesis of sound economics and human values which would make economics the servant, and not the master, of society has been made in the modern welfare state, the main achievement of national democracy. We stand now on the threshold of a new era, an era of international democracy, which will bring about the international welfare community—a projection of the concepts and ideas of the welfare state on a global scale.

If the problem of the underdeveloped nations is tackled by Keynesian methods, it lends itself to solution. The approach to the question of transfer of resources should be, first and foremost, one of economic analysis dealing with real resources; only later would the financial technicalities be dealt with. So far, the reality has not lived up to the expectation, nor has it conformed with these basic principles. The Economic and Social Council of the United Nations has expressed a somewhat pessimistic view of the results of the "development decade":

In the first half of the United Nations Development Decade— the decade of the 1960's—progress has been uneven and ultimate goals remain distant. . . . The progress thus far achieved towards the objectives of the Decade is less impressive than the fact that these objectives, although not very ambitious, remain quite distant. . . . Many of the proposals for action put forward by the Secretary-General in the summer of 1962 have hardly begun to be translated into reality, and hopes for increased resources underlying some of the proposals have not yet materialized.[2]

Thus we live in a divided world, in a period of exaggerated contrasts, with two-thirds of humanity experiencing dire distress while one-third experiences an unprecedented upsurge in its material well-being. My purpose here is to contribute, in a modest way, to the construction of a bridge between, on the one hand, the new economics and realities of the situation and, on the other, economic and political action toward the implementation of a policy of metamorphosis and change. In this sense, economics cannot be separated from value judgments, for the solution of such a problem demands an attitude inspired by a sense of history.

CONTENTS

HEMISPHERES NORTH AND SOUTH

CHAPTER 1

THE HAVES AND
THE HAVE-NOTS

There is a marked divergence in economic conditions and standards of living between the industrialized and the less developed countries of the world. It is the acutest problem of our time and in its gravity transcends all other contemporary social and economic issues. The older vertical conflict between social classes, found within every nation, is now less sharp. Today, the differentiation and disparity between rich and poor is geographical and is projected horizontally. It is the discrepancy between the industrialized and developed countries of the North and the poor and underdeveloped countries of the South.

This observation is clearly mirrored in the fact that "of the aggregate national income of all the countries that are members of the International Monetary Fund, the share of the most industrialized countries, the United States, Western Europe, and Japan, is about 75 per cent, while their share of total population is only about 25 per cent. Thus, the share of national income of the primary producing countries is 25 per cent, and their share of population is about 75 per cent."[1]

The composition of the underdeveloped two-thirds of humanity reveals itself in the following data:

There are now in 1965 about 3,300 million people in the world. Almost 1,000 million live in very poor countries; about 1,100 million in poor countries; nearly 400 million in middle-income countries; and only 800 million in rich countries.[2]

The 800 million or so inhabitants of the rich countries produce every year about seventeen times as much as the 1,000 million or so inhabitants of the very poor countries. The United States with less than 200 million people produces almost twice as much as all the 2,500 million people in the non-rich countries.

The average person in a very poor country has an income of about $85 a year; the average person in a rich country, about $1,750 a year; the average person in the United States[,] about $3,000 a year.

Every year the population of the very poor and the poor countries combined goes up by about 50 million. This is at the rate of 2.3 per cent a year. The population of the rich countries goes up at about half that rate—1.2 per cent a year.[3]

Moreover, almost half of the world's population is still hungry, or badly nourished, or both. The recent conference of the United Nations Food and Agricultural Organization presented the world with a frightening specter of famine in many underdeveloped countries within the next ten years, as the rapidly rising population of the poor nations outstrips the increase in food supply. In some of the developing countries, production of food in relation to population has actually been declining for the last five years. The reasons for this disastrous retrogression are evident:

> The food problem itself is not new; it has always existed. It is the magnitude of the problem that has changed. Two factors are responsible. First, the number of people in the world is increasing so rapidly that it now seems quite likely that the *increase* in world population between now and the end of this century, only 36 years hence, will equal or exceed the current population. Secondly, this is occurring at a time when the amount of new land suitable for cultivation is rapidly diminishing.[4]

The famine that afflicts large areas of Asia, particularly India, throws the problem into sharp relief in human terms. The following words of the President of the United States foreshadow the dangers and difficulties inherent in the situation: "Candor requires that I warn you that the time is not far off when all the combined production on all the acres of all of the agriculturally productive nations will not meet the food needs of the developing nations unless present trends are changed."[5]

Destitution, malnutrition, and distressingly low standards of living are aggravated by psychological and sociological conditions. The "demonstration effect" of modern civilization and of standards of living superior to those of the overwhelming majority of the people in underdeveloped countries is conveyed to the latter by the media of mass communication—radio, motion pictures, etc. The sociopolitical repercussions of the gap between the two major areas of the world, that is to say, between the industrialized and the underdeveloped areas, are thus magnified. The industrialized sector now faces the urgent challenge of either mitigating these politically explosive frictions and antagonisms or of taking the consequences, which may be serious. A new approach to the interrelationship between the developed and the underdeveloped parts of the world has become inevitable. The affluent sector of the world cannot remain a quiet island in the midst of a stormy ocean, an oasis of prosperity in a desert of desperate poverty.

It is natural that the tribal family in a remote corner of Africa or rural India, having lived for ages in appalling poverty, should be stimulated to claim for itself a better standard of living. There is a rising demand for a share in the wealth of the world. Even under conditions little short of starvation, the problem is no longer purely physical or biological but has taken on a sociopolitical aspect. The sole radio receiver in the village, the rare visit to a movie, the shining motor car passing through an Asian or African village convey the message of a fuller and easier life, beyond the bare struggle for existence, and under conditions that free for other uses much of the vitality now subordinated to the dreary task of keeping body and soul together. This desire to rise above the vegetative level of life is a powerful element of ferment and expectation. The conflict becomes, therefore, what has been described as a "revolution of rising expectations," and crisis has become well-nigh inevitable.

This "revolution" is, of course, fraught with illusion. The paradise of a western standard of living seems within easy reach, but the grim realities of the situation soon reveal themselves. Acquiescence in conditions of misery and poverty is gone, and the next move remains a mystery. It is true that, given modern technology and the great accumulation of wealth in the western industrialized countries, it should be possible by importation of capital to shorten the distance which the underdeveloped countries have to travel to reach the stage of self-perpetuating and self-sustained growth. But even so, the distance is long, and the road to development and modern standards is strewn with pitfalls and difficulties. There is no short cut to a better life. Tremendous efforts and a long, difficult period of transition are unavoidable.

Awareness of the possibilities and impatience with the present situation lie at the root of the revolution of rising expectations and are leading to a tragic conflict. The explosiveness of these feelings has been most strikingly reflected in events in the Congo, Laos, Vietnam, and Santo Domingo. There is potential for similar conflicts in many other countries of Asia, Africa, and Latin America. The Western world has reached the point where new instruments must be designed to promote the development of underdeveloped nations, with the clear objective of reducing the most serious and glaring examples of the gap between the industrialized and wealthy North and the underdeveloped South of the globe.

A publication of the World Bank defines the situation as follows:

> In the last 15 years the total production of goods and services in the low-income countries has increased at about the same rate as in rich countries, at about 4 per cent a year. This is a great accomplishment. But it does not mean much for the average man, woman or child in the average low-income country. In the

first place, even if production per head were to go up at the same rate in rich countries and in low-income countries, say at 4 per cent a year, this would mean an increase of about $120 per head every year in the United States but only about $3.50 per head in India. Secondly, the same rate of increase in total production in rich countries and low-income countries does not mean the same rate of increase in production per head[,] for the population of low-income countries has been increasing twice as rapidly as the population of rich countries. In the past 15 years the population of low-income countries has gone up by about two-fifths; the population of rich countries by about one-fifth. The population of the very poor members of the World Bank is now increasing at a rate of about 2.5 per cent a year, the population of the rich members of the Bank by about 1.2 per cent a year.

The result is that in the rich countries average income per head is going up by about $50 a year, in the poor countries by about $2.50 a year and in the very poor countries by about $1.50 a year. Moreover, in the past ten years the trend in the rate of growth of population in the low-income countries has been upward and the trend in the rate of growth of production has been downward so that the rate of growth in income per head has been shrinking.

If aid from rich countries to low-income countries is to be decisive, the rich countries must pour into the low-income countries a much greater flow of men, materials and skills. They must provide more of their aid on easy terms. They must open their markets much wider to the goods of the low-income countries. They must have patience for a long pull. Patience not for a decade of development but for a generation.[6]

Economic growth, however, is primarily a function of investment. Of course, investment is conceived here in its broadest meaning, that is, the investment of capital and skill, of know-how, of managerial ability, and of initiative. In every field of economic endeavor, investment is the key to progress and expansion. The most impressive example of the truth of the statement is agriculture. To expand agriculture and augment the supply of food is the most urgent concern of the underdeveloped world. Yet with the amount of uncultivated land that can be brought under tillage constantly dwindling, progress in this direction is overwhelmingly dependent on larger yields per unit of land, which can be realized only by irrigation, soil improvement, adequate use of fertilizers, and the like, all of them dependent upon input of capital.

The development of manufactures in countries which as yet have no major industries is certainly the function of import and of formation of capital and of skill, as well as of the availability of technological knowledge. There is, however, a remarkable gap between investment in the rich and in the poorer lands. In the underdeveloped parts of the world (excluding China), inhabited by 1.3 billion people, where the need is most pressing, the gross capital investment aggregated $26.9 billion, and net capital investment, after deduction of depreciation, $10 billion. In the developed part of the world, with a population of 505.8 million, gross investment was $162.4 billion, and net investment was $82.7 billion. Per capita gross capital investment in developing countries amounted to $21 per year, and net capital investment per capita was $8, as against $321 and $164, respectively, in developed countries.[7]

These are frightening figures. As economic growth is, to a considerable degree, the function of investment, so that investment is the potential of growth, the projection for the future is of a widening differential in standards of living. Not only does the accepted notion of the developing world's catching up with the progress of the developed world become totally without basis in fact, but this predicament can have other sinister implications.

The spectacle of such glaring inequality in investment is more eloquent than any other argument or exposition of the case for encouraging the economic growth of the developing nations by means of large-scale investment and influx of capital. It is surely a paradox that the rate of investment is so high in countries with overheated economies, shortages of workers, bottlenecks in productive capacity, and inflationary trends, and yet so limited in countries with dormant factors of production—in particular, the manpower left idle in the aftermath of rural unemployment or underemployment and unused natural resources.

The order of priorities is inverted, and the underdeveloped countries are caught in a scissors, of which one blade is economic crisis and famine, and the other, revolution and war.

This fateful problem is a repetition, on a global scale, of a similar drama in the history of the developed nations, which came about because of the tremendous gap between the masses of the people and the small elite of wealth, property, and privilege in Europe and America in the eighteenth and nineteenth centuries. This gap is now rapidly narrowing as a result of awakening social conscience and the strong pressure of democratic forces. The conception of the welfare state in North America, western Europe, and some other parts of the world has eased tensions, solved some social problems, and narrowed the gap in material conditions to a tolerable size. Now, however, a similar gap has been projected on a global scale, with immense effects on the political, economic, and social relations among the nations of the world. Moreover, this gap is widening and is being intensified by the growing awareness of the peoples of the developing nations of another, happier life in the developed world.

We are confronted by disparities which determine the shape of the world in which we are living today and the shape of the world of tomorrow. The first disparity, already mentioned, is that between the standard of living of the developed and of the underdeveloped sections of humanity, a disparity which, at the extremes, can be as large as thirty to one in average income. The second disparity is that between the political independence and power of the developing states, which today form the majority of the members of the United Nations and which can in some measure shape the destiny of the world, and the deplorable economic conditions existing in such states. A third disparity is that between the challenge which this problem presents and the response to it, which bears almost no relationship to the great objectives of human progress.

THE POLITICS OF INEQUALITY

As a result of these imbalances, the world is seething with unrest, and Asia, Africa, and Latin America are explosive. In less than twenty-five years India, Indonesia, Indochina, Burma, Ceylon, Israel, Ghana, Nigeria, Tunisia, Morocco, the French colonies, the Congo, Cyprus, and many other countries in East and West Africa and Southeast Asia have won independence, in some cases after violent struggle, in others after the voluntary abdication of their imperial masters. The few exceptions, for the most part, are territories where the problem is complicated by the presence in the country of a large minority of settlers from the country of the ruling power.

Despite the achievements in military technology and the enormous military superiority of Western nations, the use of the military machine to preserve and perpetuate colonial domination has become a rare occurrence, and the voluntary transfer of power to the peoples of colonial territories is today more the rule than the exception. However, the position of the West in these free but underdeveloped countries has been weakened by the attachment of the former colonial powers to the social, political, and economic *status quo*. In the international arena there are many forces discontented with the *status quo* and strongly attracted to the dynamic power of the East, with its proclamation of the need for radical change and reform. The newly independent peoples are in no position to determine whether the totalitarian challenge represents real progress or whether there are other and better ways, involving less sacrifice, of reaching the desired goal. The West has insisted, over a long period, on the maintenance of the *status quo* and has attempted to prove that the expansion of the Eastern bloc and its penetration into new areas in effect represent acts of aggression. This attitude frequently has been linked with active support for established social and economic patterns in the state concerned.

These tendencies have undergone radical change during the last few years. The historic vote of the United States on Angola, the support of democratic and progressive forces in various underdeveloped countries, the clear rejection of colonialism, the economic assistance given to underdeveloped nations, and the tolerant attitude towards neutralism—all this is helping to change the image of the West in the underdeveloped countries. But to refrain from colonial policies is not alone a sufficient remedy. There is a functional connection between peace and prosperity. Internal political instability and constant brushfire wars in the newly independent countries certainly could be reduced by a more positive Western investment in peace. But this, so far, is not what is happening, and constructive action is becoming imperative.

The crucial problem of development in the emerging countries is, in its very essence, political. These nations are deeply indoctrinated with the idea of the struggle against "colonialism." Although colonialism as a system of economic exploitation by means of political domination is today a dead issue, and the industrialized nations, with few exceptions, have found it well worth their while to disengage themselves from colonial liabilities (Britain, the Netherlands, and France are good examples), the emotional idea of anticolonialism is as alive as ever. It represents one of the great myths of our time and is a formidable political and spiritual force.

In this century, economic imperialism has outlived its usefulness. In practice, any advantage the possession of colonies may at one time have had for the metropolitan country involved has as good as disappeared. The loss of Indonesia did not in any way impair the viability of the Netherlands, whose subsequent economic recovery was one of the most spectacular in Europe.

West Germany, of course, which has no colonies at all, represents the most striking instance of economic recovery since the end of World War II.

Colonialism, then, is dead as an important factor in the life of European nations. (Of course, it never played any significant role in the economic life of the United States.) Any resistance to the emancipation of the underdeveloped nations which may still exist in the highly industrialized states which once controlled colonial empires is being undermined, not only by ideological erosion, through the progress of democracy and humanism and the political considerations inherent in the cold war, but also by the economic futility of colonialism.

In short, the political liberation of colonial countries is approaching its conclusive stage. However, the old notions of colonialism and anticolonialism still cast their shadows over the next historical goal. That goal will be one of economic growth and development in co-operation with, and by a flow of capital from, the industrialized nations. Unfortunately, the road to that goal is obstructed by an undergrowth of political ideologies and conceptions produced by quite different economic and social conditions. Inertia is largely responsible for this, and is likely to continue until the new trends behind economic and social change become the subject of realistic and acceptable analysis.

The two stages of liberation—the political and the socioeconomic—are fundamentally different in their policy requirements but are frequently confused by the people of the underdeveloped countries. It is possible to distinguish between these widely differing stages in the historical development of the former colonial countries and to put an end to the confusion which bedevils relations between the industrialized and underdeveloped areas of the world only through a concrete demonstration of speedy economic growth, with a consequent rise in the standard of living, in the underdeveloped nations.

With the rapid political emancipation of colonial countries in the twentieth century, the anachronistic character of colonialism became evident. This was borne out most strikingly in the speech of the late Prime Minister of India, Nehru, at the conference of uncommitted nations in Belgrade. On that occasion, Nehru expressed the view that colonialism had ceased to be an important problem in our time and that, indeed, practical concern with colonialism was no longer meaningful or useful, but had become more or less an example of flogging a dead horse.

However, what the former colonial countries want is not only freedom from domination and fear but also freedom from want, hunger, and economic insecurity. In the last decade, demographic expansion in the underdeveloped countries accelerated side by side with a worsening of economic conditions due to the decline in the prices of primary products. Under these conditions, the nations liberated from colonial regimes developed high expectations, with, of course, political independence at the top of the list. But political independence and sovereignty were not enough to solve fundamental economic and social problems. They could do but little to prevent further stagnation and an increasing decline in the standard of living. Slogans left over from the struggle against imperialism were seized upon as substitutes for practical measures to ease an economic and social distress that was rapidly becoming more and more grave. It is significant, therefore, that at a time when the political liberation of colonial countries was taking place at a faster rate than at any other period in history, the nations thus freed had to fall back on anti-imperialist slogans as a kind of outlet for their deep disappointment with the reality of their sovereignty and dawning national maturity.

The struggle of these nations for economic viability and independence, however, has little, if any, relevance to the old notions of anticolonialism. In such a struggle, not further disengagement but a deeper involvement of industrialized states in the development and economic growth of the underdeveloped nations is required. Not only independence but also a much greater degree of interdependence is called for.

THE PROBLEMS OF INEQUALITY

Production. The disparities that lie at the root of the economic problems of our time are paradoxical. In the highly developed countries shortage of demand slows down production and from time to time creates situations in which production capacity in many fields is less than fully utilized. In the underdeveloped countries, on the other hand, production lags well behind minimum needs.

In agriculture, productivity is lagging where its increase is most imperative and, in relative terms, is lowest where the agricultural population is the highest. Increases in agricultural production are most common where stocks of food are already excessive. Growth of population, up to the level of an explosion, is most pronounced where malnutrition prevails. Countries most in need of capital investment have the least. The rate of saving is lowest where new investments are most urgently required, and this for the simple reason that adequate saving is more or less out of the question where incomes are at, or below, the subsistence level.

In trying to evaluate the progress made along the tortuous road toward improvement of the standard of living in developing nations, we should mention the following statement by the World Bank:

> Now, in order to evaluate whether this 4 per cent [of economic growth] has been much or little, it is not enough to refer back to past history and say it is more than ever happened before—because as we have seen nothing happened before— but we have to relate it to some kind of objective criterion. In order to do that you have to relate first the growth rate of 4 per cent to the population growth which, of course, offsets to a considerable extent this accomplishment. Population growth in the underdeveloped parts of the world has in recent years been running at a rate of something like 2 per cent, or perhaps a bit higher. So we are left with a rate of income growth per capita of 1½ per cent on the average.

The question then is whether this 1½ per cent per capita growth rate is adequate. The answer is a matter of judgment—judgment as to what is considered a "significant" rate of growth: what do people feel when their family income goes up by 1, or 1½, or 2 per cent per year?

One way of looking at this problem is to see how long it takes for a family, for a social class, for a group, to achieve a doubling of its income. You can read in any compound interest table that a 1 per cent rate requires approximately 70 years to double in income. Well, I suggest that 70 years is too long a time to wait for such doubling of income. It takes almost three generations. There, 1 per cent would not be enough.[8]

In analyzing these figures, it should be kept in mind that what is involved here is an increase in the level of national income per head from some $100 to about $200.

In the same publication, the following remarks are pertinent to this subject:

In many underdeveloped countries the agricultural sector has been sadly lagging behind, to the point that in a number of countries an agricultural production per capita is smaller than it was 10 or 15 years ago. Depending upon which of the latest reports you read, you find that food production the world over has just about kept pace with the population growth or, according to some more pessimistic estimates[,] food production has already fallen behind the population growth. . . .

These statistics show that in the last 20 years world trade has expanded at a rate never before achieved and that we now have much more international trade than we ever had before. But they also show that most of the expansion has taken place in trade between the advanced countries and from the advanced countries to the underdeveloped countries, while exports from the underdeveloped countries have not significantly risen. . . . They now have what the people concerned with debt service call a "debt bulge." Over the next three years some of the countries I have in mind face the prospects of having to set aside something like 25 to 30 per cent of their foreign exchange earnings to meet their debt service obligations.[9]

This situation is fraught with grave dangers, and its tragedy is that the dangers are so easily avoidable. For the first time in history, existing technological and economic knowledge is equal to the task of increasing production faster than population everywhere in the world.

Population. Population growth, the terms of trade, and the absence of adequate capital formation in less developed countries, as well as the paucity of capital imports, all combine to aggravate the human, political, and economic factors which go to make up a major world problem. Despite modern technological advance and the wealth of many countries, there are more poverty-stricken people throughout the world now than there were fifty or a hundred years ago.

The disparity in economic standards and in stages of economic development is aggravated by demography. The specter evoked by Malthus is walking again. Frequently, development is unable to catch up with the rapid increase of population. Standards of living in countries of limited resources and extreme population pressure cannot be further depressed without grave consequences. We are living in the period of demographic explosion. At the present rate of increase, the world population will double every forty-two years and will amount to some six billion by the end of this century.

The pressure of growing populations on scarce resources is accentuated, of course, in countries that are already densely populated. This is seen clearly by comparing the average rate of net increase in population of industrialized areas (0.9 in Europe, 1.7 in North America) with that of underdeveloped areas (2.3 in Africa, 2.3 in Asia, 2.8 in Central and South America), where the pressure on limited resources is the greatest. Thus, in some of the underdeveloped areas of the globe the population grew by 25 per cent in the last decade, and the growth rate is apparently still climbing. In such areas the standard of living is already at, or below, subsistence level and cannot be further depressed without grave political, social, and economic consequences.

The population of Asia, excluding the U.S.S.R., is increasing at a rate of some 35 millions per annum, in comparison with an increase of about 9 millions in the Americas and 4 millions in Europe (again excluding the U.S.S.R.).

A paradox appears in this demographic discrepancy: the more extensive and organized the health services and hygiene, the graver the population problem. In such areas the main factor in the rapid increase of the population is not so much the rise in birth rate as the decline in the mortality rate, which in some underdeveloped countries dropped 30 to 60 per cent in one decade. In certain countries there is the highest rate of reproduction known in human history, with the population doubling every twenty-two to twenty-five years. Preventive medicine, improved methods of hygiene, and an increasing use of vaccination, sulfa drugs, and antibiotics, and of DDT to prevent the spread of malaria, are radically reducing the mortality rate, particularly among infants. While the death rate is falling rapidly, the birth rate continues to be high.

This extraordinary increase in population occurs in the underdeveloped nations in spite of appalling poverty and low living standards, which, in India for example, are reflected in a life expectancy of forty-five years for males, and forty-seven years for females (the figures for 1957–58). This contrasts with some sixty-five to seventy-five years in the developed countries of Europe and America. In countries in which the decline in the death rate is gradual, there are, as a rule, simultaneous changes in mental, psychological, and cultural attitudes which bring about a decline in the birth rate. It is obvious, however, that where the decline in the mortality rate is rapid social changes cannot keep pace, so that the decline in the birth rate lags behind the decline in the death rate. In these instances production cannot keep up with the population increase, and the standard of living, therefore, does not rise. Moreover, changes in the birth rate through conscious control of procreation are subject to cultural and psychological, as well as social and religious, pressures, and such pressures are generally of a rigid and conservative nature.

Eugene Black, former president of the World Bank, warned recently that all the efforts of industrial countries would be negated if populations in the poorer countries continued to grow at their present rate of 2 to 3.5 per cent yearly. He maintained that to point to the supposedly favorable economic effect of a growing population is "widely irrelevant" to the problems facing most developing countries today: "We are coming to a situation in which the optimist will be the man who thinks that present living standards can be maintained."[10] These circumstances explain the efforts of the underdeveloped nations to exorcise the Malthusian demon as a precondition to the raising of living standards. If they do not, any increase in the gross national product may be counterbalanced by a similar increase in population.

The vicious circle of an uncontrolled demographic expansion and a declining standard of living is closing. The disproportion in standards of living between one part of the world and another is steadily worsening and is being accentuated by growing differences in per capita income. Under these circumstances, governments in countries with rapidly expanding populations and limited resources tend to promote plans to slow down the population increase. They are ready to resort to birth control as a national policy, with a view to preventing mass starvation and unemployment on an ever-increasing scale.

The committee appointed by the World Bank to study development problems in India and Pakistan, the members of which were Sir Oliver Franks, Mr. Allan Sproul, and Mr. Hermann Abs, summarized this situation in the following way:

It is true that Governments have endorsed programs of education in family planning, though the results of this may not be realized for some time. Moreover, as the populations of both countries achieve a higher degree of literacy, and become more aware of the possibilities of achieving an improved standard of life, the present trend towards smaller families in the urban areas may become more widespread. However, it is impossible to say when a significant fall in the birth rate will occur, and in the meantime both Governments are confronted with the task of providing the extra food and other necessities required by increase in population of the order of 18 to 20 per cent over the next ten years, while at the same time struggling to bring about an increase in *per capita* income.[11]

In China a few years ago an initial acceptance of birth control was followed by a dogmatic suppression of all efforts in this direction. However, famine, along with the failure of certain economic policies, has compelled even the most dogmatic of the Communist regimes to modify its ideology and to adopt a more flexible demographic approach. The new attitude toward birth control, with its reversal of the expansionist population policy, is a most significant deviation from rigid orthodoxy and one of great importance, given the demographic and economic conditions prevailing in China.

The most effective remedy for the frightening erosion of economic standards and the political dangers arising out of it is the conscious determining of the demographic process itself, by means of birth control and family planning. Thus, the human will again interferes with one of the most complex phenomena of individual and social life. "Family planning," as it is euphemistically called, is tantamount to intruding upon the laws of nature. This willful encroachment on the realm of nature, especially when it is made official policy, may have the deepest and most formidable impact on human destiny. The idea that it may be a better investment to limit natural increase than to encourage it by expanding the supply of capital goods and equipment is gaining ground in underdeveloped countries.

These policies are supported by such logical reasoning as that expressed in an address delivered by Arnold Toynbee at a conference of the United Nations Food and Agricultural Organization:

> Our efforts to reduce the death-rate must be paralleled by conscious efforts to keep the birth-rate under control; for the resources of this planet, even if scientifically administered and

developed and husbanded for the benefit of the whole human
family, will not suffice forever to feed a population that is
increasing *ad infinitum*. We may select the most desirable crops
and livestock and raise them on the soils suited to them; we may
cultivate the sea, as the Japanese have begun to do. But, sooner
or later, food production will reach its limit; and then, if population is still increasing, famine will do the execution that was done
in the past by famine, pestilence, and war combined. . . . All
over the world until lately, and in most of the world still today,
mankind, in its sexual life, has been following the course of Nature; that is to say, it has been breeding up to the maximum. To
let Nature take her extravagant course in the reproduction of the
human race may have made sense in an age in which we were
also letting her take her course in decimating mankind by the
casualties of war, pestilence, and famine. Being human, we have
at last revolted against that senseless waste. We have started to
impose on Nature's heartless play a humane new order of our
own. But, when once man has begun to interfere with Nature,
he cannot afford to stop half way. We cannot, with impunity, cut
down the death-rate and at the same time allow the birth-rate to
go on taking Nature's course. We must consciously try to
establish an equilibrium or, sooner or later, famine will stalk
abroad again.[12]

However, so far, only one Asian country has succeeded in
slowing down the growth of its population. Using every available
means, ranging from birth control to abortion, Japan, industrially
and educationally the most progressive country in Asia, although
poorly endowed with natural resources, has managed to decrease
its birth rate. In that country the drop in the birth rate averaged
43 per cent for the period 1945–49 to 1963. While in the prewar
years the population of Japan had increased at an average annual
rate of 12.3 per thousand, in the postwar period it showed a
downward trend, until today it is only 9.0 per thousand per
year.

Trade. Another economic disparity is produced by the price
pattern, and especially the price fluctuations, of a modern
economy. The changes in the prices of primary commodities as a

group have been much greater than those of manufactured goods as a group. While the prices of manufactured products have been maintained and in many industries have risen, the prices of primary products have steadily declined. This fact has created balance of payment difficulties for the primary producing countries, particularly in view of their fixed obligations. The decline reflects long-term structural trends and does not arise only in connection with general cyclical fluctuations in the world economy. We are faced with some basic structural changes.

In the report submitted to the United Nations Conference on Trade and Development (UNCTAD), which took place in Geneva in March to June, 1964, the *loss* caused the developing nations by the terms of trade was estimated at *17 per cent* over a period of eleven years. On this point there is a striking comment by Dr. Raúl Prebisch, Secretary-General of UNCTAD, in the introduction to the report submitted to him by a group of experts: "The Geneva Conference of 1964 had pointed to the obstacles to development that result from the structural imbalance in world trade, and particularly from the fact that world demand for the primary commodities exported by developing countries is growing much more slowly than the essential import requirements of these countries, taking into account the need for an acceleration in their rates of growth."[13]

The report itself says: "Expansion of world trade in the last decade and a half has to a large extent by-passed the developing countries. The share of developing countries in world exports has fallen from nearly a third in 1950 to a fifth in 1964. The terms of trade have also moved against them with the result that the capacity of developing countries to import out of export earnings has grown less than the volume of their exports."[14]

A study made by the International Monetary Fund attributes this difference between the two types of countries to

the greater price instability of primary as compared with manufactured exports, which in turn results both from the relatively inelastic demand and supply conditions characteristic of most primary products and from the relatively unstable conditions affecting the supply of many products of agricultural origin. While in the case of manufactured exports, demand fluctuations usually affect their volume rather than their prices, in the case of most primary exports the opposite is true.

Data on export prices for the periods 1929–38 and 1950–58 compiled by the League of Nations and the Statistical Office of the United Nations reveal that, in each of the two periods, average year-to-year changes in the prices of primary products as a group were some 50 to 55 per cent greater than those of manufactures as a group.[15]

The fact is that the developing nations are caught in the gap between the declining prices of primary products and the rising prices of capital equipment and manufactured goods. This decline in prices of primary products reflects long-term structural trends connected with certain technological developments, which have diminished the value of raw materials in the final manufactured product and have introduced many synthetic products as substitutes for natural materials:

> Over the last ten years, industrial production in the Western world has been expanding at a rate of almost 5 per cent per annum, and the volume of imports of the industrialized countries by 6 per cent. On the other hand, the exports of the primary producing countries have risen in volume by only a little over 3 per cent per annum, and the real value of these exports—in terms of their power to purchase imports—by just over 2 per cent. In large measure, these developments have been the result of certain technical aspects of recent economic growth. Thus, in the highly industrialized countries, expansion of output has been heavily concentrated on more complicated manufactured goods, such as machinery, electrical goods, aircraft, etc., with a relatively low raw material content, which has limited the demand for raw materials. The more effective use of materials, perhaps most strikingly illustrated by the tin-saving process of electrolytic plating, has had a similar effect. In addition, the substitution of synthetics for raw materials, which has been rapidly spreading in many of the major branches of manufacturing, has been of great importance—the use of plastics, deter-

gents, synthetic fibers, and synthetic rubber, to mention just a
few. The immediate impact of these changes is no doubt
unfavorable to raw material exporters, at least during a transitional period, but they are part of the technological progress of
our times.[16]

One important change of great significance for the industrial
regions is the gradual decline in recent years in *the average
amount of raw materials and fuels required* per unit of
manufacturing production. To give an example: a locomotive
producing 50 per cent. more motive power than its counterpart
did in 1920 weighs now only half as much. In the annual report
of G. A. T. T., published in May 1956, it is shown that in 1938
the ratio between the amount of raw materials and fuels
consumed and the gross value of manufacturing production in
industrial areas was 25 per cent.; by 1955 it had dropped to 17½
per cent. Moreover, the industrial areas are able to produce
more raw materials themselves, especially those of a synthetic
kind: rayon, aluminium, synthetic rubber, plastic materials, etc.
The raw-material-producing countries, on the other hand, are
manufacturing more of their textiles themselves. While, in
absolute terms, trade between the industrial and the non-
industrial parts of the world has been well maintained and has
even expanded somewhat in recent years, it is in trade between
industrial areas that the most conspicuous rise has occurred, and
there has consequently been a relative decline in trade between
the industrial and the non-industrial parts of the world.[17]

In 1964, export prices of agricultural commodities fell by an
average of 12 per cent. The decline was concentrated in
commodities on which the developing countries depend, such as
sugar, coffee, and fibers. Since 1951, the underlying trend of
world prices of primary commodities, measured in the aggregate,
has been irregularly but steeply downward. The situation at the
end of 1965 has been described as follows: "The soft under belly
of world trade this year is the primary producers. These
countries' payments had begun to weaken last year. The deterioration continued into the early months of 1965. It has now
reached the point where some primary producers have already
had to take action to restrict the rise in their imports. Others will

undoubtedly follow. And the industrial countries in their turn will feel the backwash on their exports."[18]

A further expansion in the production of raw materials for internal use in countries producing primary commodities is impossible, if only because declining living standards prevent the consumption of these materials at a rate equal to the increase of population. For at least the last three decades, the underdeveloped areas of the world have, in fact, substantially raised their share in the production, and lowered their share in the consumption, of primary commodities.

Even in times of boom in the highly developed industrial countries, there was no improvement in the terms of trade for the underdeveloped nations. The decline in prices has a cumulative effect because such declines discourage large stock holdings, the disposal of which further depresses the already downward trend of prices.

The demand of the underdeveloped nations for stabilizing measures such as buffer stocks of primary commodities is thus supported by strong arguments, which emphasize, on the one hand, the great benefit derived by the industrialized nations from the downward trend of prices, and, on the other, the well-nigh intolerable burden thus imposed on the underdeveloped nations, with their basic problem of overpopulation, their heavy debt obligations, and so on. Any stabilizing measures are, however, only palliatives. They are not adequate to reverse the trend of steady deterioration.

CHAPTER 2

FACTORS IN
ECONOMIC GROWTH

The current trends in demography and terms of trade, with all their economic implications, are aggravated by sociological and psychological factors arising from the impact of modern civilization. It has already been pointed out that the larger national income in the highly developed and mature economies of Europe and the western hemisphere, the high level of consumption, and the tendency to consume conspicuously are conveyed to the underdeveloped countries through modern methods of mass communication and have widespread social and economic repercussions. They create new desires by displaying economic and social conditions hitherto virtually unknown in backward countries. Attempts to utilize existing resources and to mobilize new ones, with a view to accelerating the process of economic development in the underdeveloped states, become imperative under these circumstances. Economic growth becomes a supreme policy aim to which all other objectives are subordinated.

AGRICULTURAL PRODUCTIVITY

The self-perpetuating forces of economic growth can be released only by greater productivity. However, malnutrition and food shortages in underdeveloped countries are powerful enemies of rising productivity and therefore of economic development generally. The caloric intake per person per day, which ranges between 3,000 and 3,300 in the industrialized countries of Europe and America, is less than 2,000 in India and Pakistan.

Productivity in agriculture is increasing slowly where its rapid increase is most imperative. In relative terms it is at its lowest where the proportion of the population engaged in agriculture is highest. There is a marked disparity of income in most of these nations. In almost every country the agricultural worker's income is substantially below the average national income per capita, and differentials as great as 77 per cent exist.

The social contradictions which in the past provided the fertile soil of wars and revolutions are now projected onto the global scene and are likely to increase the danger of a world conflict. These contradictions, disparities, and paradoxical developments are, however, susceptible to change and reversal by conscious and sustained human effort. Given reasonable progress in control of population size, with a slowing down of rapid and unlimited growth, the introduction of modern economic methods can raise the standard of living even in relatively overpopulated countries. Under a "managed" economy subject to rapid changes in technical processes, with increasing productivity both in agriculture and industry, and fluctuations in the economic equilibrium, the conception of overpopulation and underpopulation becomes relative and vague. The view that certain factors influencing distribution of population and standards of living can be placed, in part at least, under human control has been confirmed by experience.

The capacity of a country to sustain its population is today an undefined and hardly definable concept. It is doubtful that it can ever be measured in fixed, arithmetic terms. It is the function of a large number of variables, and these variables depend, in turn, on the particular experience of each country. Transformation of economic conditions, technical discoveries and inventions, development of potential resources, shifts in consumption and in marketing facilities, as well as such variable elements as capital supply and scientific and technical knowledge, are subject to almost unceasing change, which can be brought about by one or more factors. The level of cultural and technical development of a country is one obvious influence. The economic and social system, the structure and quality of the population, and the occupational distribution are other such influences; where, as in most instances, there are several of these factors at work, their dynamic interaction is itself important.

An analysis of the economic history of various countries shows that population density differs radically from country to country as a result of human activity rather than natural conditions. The location of centers of production is not fixed. Changes in productivity, particularly in agriculture, are frequently an effect of artificial conditions brought about by economic, political, or other national policies.

The level of agricultural productivity, the degree of industrialization, the occupational distribution—these all seem to be factors determining, to a great extent, not only the economic situation of a country but also its population density. For that matter, the incidents of national life that come under the general heading of history, and which include political, social, constitutional, and ethnic considerations, play their part in determining which areas shall be densely and which sparsely inhabited. Geography alone has never provided a satisfactory explanation of the difference in population density between one area and another. Today the forces of history (whose importance is increasing) and the forces of nature (whose importance is decreasing) are the factors which determine, within certain physical limits, a country's capacity to sustain its population and to raise its standard of living. The tendency toward the emancipation of population potentialities from close dependence on natural resources has been reinforced by the developments of the machine age. Modern economic development inevitably influences the capacity of a country to support its population. The almost physiocratic idea of such capacity, which puts it into an extremely close relationship with available space and natural resources, does not conform to the economic conditions now prevailing.

Since agriculture has ceased to be the major occupation in progressive communities, the importance of such natural resources in estimating the economic potential of a country has diminished. Many new factors, physical and economic, have a direct bearing on this potential. There can no longer be any rigid limit on economic possibilities. It is important, therefore, that the relative weight and interaction of the new factors be assessed, and plans made accordingly.

Historical, economic, and social knowledge must be applied to the process of economic growth. The fact that, by comparison with the other criteria, that of physical space is receding in importance does not prove that the greater the population density, the closer the approach to an optimum number of people. A country's economic potential is a relative concept, as is demonstrated by the importance of the human factor as against natural resources. For example, the limits within which a given supply of agricultural land can support and absorb an increase in population have been greatly extended, mainly because modern methods have greatly increased productivity per acre and thereby freed agricultural production from the close and almost exclusive dependence on land area as a determinant of productivity.

Both interspatial and intertemporal comparisons go far to bear out the contention that the range between minimum and maximum yields per unit of land and differences in productivity per unit and per worker are so great as to defeat any attempt at estimating the technical and natural capacity of a country to produce an increasing volume of foodstuffs. It must be borne in mind, however, that where values are quoted in intertemporal comparisons, certain increases may represent a shift in the value of crops. They may also represent net increases in yields per unit or increases due to the substitution of higher priced crops for those formerly cultivated. In most of the cases reviewed, the extremes of low and high yields, of more and less valuable crops, and of higher and lower productivity per settler cannot be satisfactorily explained on the basis of natural conditions. The interchangeability of artificially produced and natural conditions seems to be important in this development. It should be remembered, too, that the revolutionary changes in agriculture, which brought about an increased productivity of agricultural labor, were very rapid in the period between the wars.

As has already been mentioned, another factor extending the limits within which production values may increase is the shift from less valuable to more valuable crops. The tendency to accelerate this shift is the result of two distinct but parallel processes: (a) the increase in national income of the more developed countries, both aggregate and per capita; and (b) the progress of nutritional science. Both these processes tend to promote the substitution of the more valuable, high-protein foodstuffs for the cheaper energy-producing foods, if only by bringing about a change in the relative weight of these two ingredients in the national diet.

The interaction of all these factors—the increased productivity of the soil per unit of land and per earner; the accumulation of knowledge as well as of capital; interchangeability of space, capital, and knowledge; the shift away from energy-producing to protective foodstuffs; the introduction of new crops—has had a far-reaching influence on agriculture.

INDUSTRIALIZATION

Another factor promoting a rise in the standard of living in overpopulated countries, where further population growth is being reasonably well controlled, is industrialization. The tendency of industry toward decentralization, and the far-reaching effects of its removal from dependence on local raw materials and other indigenous factors, reflects the trend of world industrial development. In the past, industry tended to concentrate in certain specially favored areas, in which a large market, transport, banking, and other facilities were available. Other factors determining the establishment of industries in certain areas were the availability of skilled labor and the presence of auxiliary industries.

Technical progress, however, has reduced the importance of these considerations. New, simplified industrial processes can easily be imitated in new countries, and shifts in consumer centers have given the impetus to the establishment of new industries in new areas. As a result of this development, industry is concentrating increasingly in areas not endowed by nature with plentiful natural resources. In industry natural resources are becoming interchangeable with capital, skill, and knowledge, and with a deliberate national policy of industrialization. Marketing facilities also are becoming a decisive factor in determining industry location.

Expanding markets reduce costs and increase the productivity of industry by facilitating the full utilization of productive capacity. At the same time, a growing population with a rising standard of living creates technical and economic minima of production and so diversifies the production of an increasing number of industrial goods.

THE LABOR FORCE

In view of the fact that in all countries the larger part of industrial production is based on domestic consumption, with only the smaller part available for export, the growth of the population becomes increasingly important, especially where such growth goes side by side with increasing purchasing power. Thus, there is one indispensable precondition for raising the standard of living in overpopulated countries: the supply of capital must keep pace with the increase in the labor force and, in the course of time, overtake it. Otherwise, the growth of population can only lead to further deterioration in the standard of living.

The shift in the relative importance of the factors determining the economic growth of a country is basic to present-day economic development. Changes in occupational distribution, which are a concomitant of the division of labor and the transition to new forms of production, influence the capacity of a country to support its population and to raise its standard of living. New population strata, resulting from the shift in occupational distribution and accretion of capital, cannot be accounted for by any estimate of cultivated land. They are the outcome of structural and socioeconomic changes which react on the whole nation, transforming it from a subsistence to an exchange economy. The idea of self-sufficiency in food is being abandoned, and trade has replaced some of the factors which used to determine the productive capacity of a given area.

Diversified demand, consequent upon higher income, has increased the share of secondary and tertiary stages of production. When productivity is increasing, there should be fewer producers in the primary stage of production; otherwise, no market would be found for their products. Thus, the alternatives are these: either many producers with low productivity, as in the backward countries, or high productivity with fewer primary producers, as in the more developed nations.

It would appear, therefore, that within the limits of controlled population growth, the capacity of a country to support its population and to raise its standard of living is to some extent a function of three factors: natural resources; skill and know-how, or the general quality of the population; and the capital available for the development of resources. Moreover, these factors are, to a very great extent, interchangeable: a country can do with fewer natural resources if it has a highly skilled labor force and ample capital equipment, and vice versa. The interchangeability of

these factors has a bearing on the whole problem of development
and growth in countries with a low standard of living and limited
resources.

The utilization of available resources is at least as important as
their availability. An increase in productivity per man per work
day would be the direct result of a more intensive utilization of
productive resources. Wherever industrial techniques and the
economy have attained a certain degree of development, wherever the population has reached a period of co-operation and
interaction, wherever the increase in population makes for a
more efficient use of natural resources, the productivity of the
individual worker increases.

The whole problem is put in a nutshell in the following
analysis:

> The size, rate of growth, and age composition of the population
> of a given area are factors bearing vitally on the appraisal of its
> resources. Population trends, however, must always be consid-
> ered in conjunction with, or in relation to, cultural development.
> Numbers of people by themselves mean little; but numbers with
> certain knowledge, endowed with certain abilities, supported by
> "horse power," handicapped by certain inhibitions, are vital.
> Moreover, population status must be considered; the treatment
> must be dynamic, not static. Growth as contrasted with stagna-
> tion or decline counts, rather than density; for growth affects the
> wants, art, and institutions in quite a different way than
> stagnation does, and rapid growth differently from slow
> growth.[1]

Of course, the evaluation of the importance of the human
material and of its training, knowledge, and skill must be made
in the broader context of the technical civilization and the
institutional organization of knowledge and research. (The so-
called "ferment of ideas" is certainly an imponderable factor
which can never be taken into account in a static conception of
economic viability.)

> Large fixed investments are represented in the special skills of
> the expert shoemaker, the designers of women's fashion, the

mining engineer, the industrial chemist, the expert farmer, the marine navigator, the bone surgeon, the maker of optical goods, the jewel cutter, the horticulturist, the architect of bridges, the irrigation engineer. . . . Finally, there is a human resource not entirely bound to any particular persons but socially carried, and institutionally preserved and fostered; knowledge, especially the systematic knowledge of science, and industrial techniques based upon it. This resource exists in libraries, in laboratories, in universities and public school systems, in the practices of office and shop and mill, in the traditions of science and the scientific spirit.

Important parts of it are in the "atmosphere" of a particular culture. Knowledge of different kinds is unevenly distributed over the earth today and probably always will be, despite rapid communications, because knowledge is highly specialized.[2]

CAPITAL

In the April, 1961, issue of *Foreign Affairs,* the thesis that capital is only one of the components essential for the progress of underdeveloped nations was summarized in the article, "A Positive Approach to Economic Aid," by John Kenneth Galbraith, as follows:

Were ample assistance all that is required, Iran and the oil-rich Arab countries would be exceedingly progressive. In fact, in these countries progress remains unsatisfactory, and it is because other requirements for advance are missing. No one supposes that, were the oil revenues of Iraq doubled, the rate of economic development would be appreciably advanced. Similarly, Venezuela, in spite of its massive oil revenues, remains in uncertain equilibrium. Nor would economic aid in larger volume have saved the situation in Cuba or Laos.[3]

However, skills alone are of no avail if capital equipment, essential in a modern economy, is not forthcoming. A rapidly growing population is in need of a constant expansion of capital equipment, of improvement of the land to provide more food-stuffs and raw materials, of additional industrial enterprises, means of communication, and so on. Thus, one of the most essential prerequisites of development is capital equipment, which serves in a developing country as a factor making for expansion of production, for "lack of capital and capital equipment is one of the causes of Eastern poverty, and one of the greatest obstacles to industrial development."[4]

Natural resources represent only the potential of a country, and their utilization depends, to a great extent, upon the availability of capital equipment. The effect of these two divergent factors on the progress of the population toward some hypothetical optimum largely depends on their quantitative relations and interactions. An increase in capital equipment should be conducive to a greater division of labor and should facilitate the transition to a capitalist form of economy. The acquisition of such equipment subjects the economic structure of a country to a dual upset. It superimposes on the old economy an industrialized system of production, increases the share of "tertiary" income (i.e., the increase in income resulting from the shift from production of goods to production of services) because of the greater division of labor, and creates new employment opportunities.

The development of a backward colonial country is impossible without large imports of capital:

The importation of large amounts of capital from metropolitan and foreign countries is the distinguishing characteristic of the development of colonial territories in modern times. The early development of colonies by settlement and trade did not require large amounts of fixed capital; but with the evolution of machine production the cost of development greatly increased, so that colonial territories became ever more dependent economically on the large industrial and commercial centres of Europe, America and the Orient. The application of capitalist methods to colonial production has made colonial communities the debtors of the investors, both public and private, of the countries which supply the capital. Colonial produce is sold in the world market, not simply in exchange for goods consumed by the colonial community, but for capital goods which enable it to produce for the world markets and so pay the interest on its borrowing.[5]

If we substitute the term "developing" for "colonial," this economic analysis is as valid today as it was in 1937.

The problem is aggravated by the demographic expansion in underdeveloped countries, which goes beyond anything which could have been envisaged only a generation ago. The relationship between the increase in population, the access to new capital, and the average unit of capital per head is directly relevant to the standard of living—its rise or decline—in an underdeveloped nation. In such a nation, with a rapidly increasing population, the process of natural accumulation of capital cannot be fast enough for an adequate expansion of productive capacity, which should keep pace with the population increase unless external capital resources are made available as loans or investments. This is because

the ability of a country to sustain an increase in population depends, not only upon the wealth of its natural resources, but also upon its capital equipment and upon the technical ability of its producers. For this reason, a relatively underdeveloped country may give signs of a temporary rural overpopulation in spite of rich natural resources, if the rate of growth of its population is more rapid than the growth of its capital equipment and the development of its industrial and agricultural technique. . . .

A large number of the countries with rapidly increasing populations are agricultural and lack capital. Such countries may be faced with serious economic problems as their population growth leads to rural overpopulation. In present conditions of restricted foreign markets, it will be difficult for them to expand their exports of agricultural products. Even if they possess raw materials, lack of capital may prevent them from exploiting these resources and from industrialising; for their own savings will probably be meagre and it will be difficult for them to borrow from abroad. . . .[6]

However, the flow of capital required for new development and for the mitigation of the stresses and strains upon the economy of an underdeveloped country as well as for raising the standard of living, encouraging international trade, and above all, expanding the productive capacity, can be derived from only two sources—capital formation through savings and accumulation, or capital import.

CHAPTER 3

ACCUMULATION
OF CAPITAL

PRIMARY FORMATION OF CAPITAL

The first Industrial Revolution was based on a very high rate of savings and a large accumulation of private capital. The distribution of the national income in those days had the effect of accelerating the formation of capital by assuring a high rate of profit. Wage rates were kept at levels just sufficient for the maintenance and reproduction of the labor force, an action that was possible because there was always a reserve army of unemployed workers to call upon. It was a dismal, grim period and well illustrated the theory of the "iron wage law." Such conditions were possible only within a society in which democratic government was in a nascent state, and most of the population was either deprived of political influence or was inarticulate.

This revolution was re-enacted in the U.S.S.R. after the 1917 revolution. The very existence of the new regime depended upon rapid economic progress. Speedy industrialization, occupational reshuffling, and large-scale urbanization were possible only by the rapid formation of capital through forced saving. That totalitarian regime was strong and stern enough to enforce such a solution, and today China is trying to achieve a similar result by forced saving and reduced consumption:

In 19th century Europe and Meiji Japan, economic development was in fact achieved by denying the impoverished majority
the means of a better life and by diverting capital savings into
the building of an industrial infrastructure. In the Soviet Union
under Stalin this formula was carried to a ruthless extreme in the
systematic regulation of every phase of economic and social
life. . . . But today we are living in a totally new political
environment in which increased literacy, modern communications and the consequent awareness of new techniques are
rapidly raising popular expectations. As a result, we may expect
to see new energies bursting up from the bottom of the social
pyramid.[1]

There is one common feature between the early capitalism of
the Industrial Revolution in England and western Europe, on the
one hand, and the economics of the Soviet regime and of China
in the postwar period, on the other. It is the rapid formation of
capital through cruel and ruthless restraint of consumption and
reduction in living standards. Such an economic policy was
possible in predemocratic days and is enforceable today by
totalitarian regimes. It led to appalling poverty among the
masses in the early capitalist society and to an extremely low
standard of living in totalitarian countries during the initial
period of their development.

It is well-nigh impossible to draw up a comparative balance
sheet of the suffering endured by the masses under the early
capitalist system in western Europe and of that experienced
under Russian communism during the period following World
War I. The number of people who perished in the early years of
the Soviet state is certainly much larger than was the direct loss
of life caused by similar conditions in the period of early
capitalism. However, one must take into account the fact that the
primary accumulation of capital in Russia had to be carried out
immediately after a devastating civil war. At the same time, of
course, it took place under much more advantageous technological conditions. The advance in productivity and technology, as
well as the many technical and other innovations inducing

increased productivity per head—particularly in agriculture—
shortened the period of extreme privation in Russia. The tractor
and combine are among the many examples of the tremendous
differences between technical conditions in the period of early
capitalism in western Europe and those in the U.S.S.R. in the
twenties and thirties. Agricultural progress was to a very great
extent made possible by these technical innovations.

Thus, the changeover from a semi-agrarian, backward economy to a high technological level was much more violent in
Communist Russia than were the similar upheavals of the early
capitalist society of western Europe. The period of extreme
destitution and privation, however, was shorter in Russia. The
maze of economic, political, and, last but not least, technological
changes from the beginning of the Industrial Revolution in
western Europe up to the forced industrialization of Russia is so
complicated and involved that it is impossible to estimate
accurately the extent to which each factor contributed in
accentuating these differences. There can be little doubt, however, that the remarkable progress in technological methods was
one of the most important factors, if not decisive, in shortening
the transition period in the U.S.S.R.

The conventional means of bringing about rapid primary
accumulation of capital in underdeveloped countries in our time
would offer almost insuperable difficulties. First and foremost,
the difficulty would be economic. While the national per capita
income in Europe averages between $500 and $1,200, in most
countries of Asia it ranges between $60 and $100. An Indian or
Egyptian village, with its emaciated inhabitants in their hovels,
has to be seen if the appalling poverty in these hundreds of
thousands of villages (amounting in India alone to some half a
million) is to be realized.

The process of primary formation of capital under such
circumstances is obviously extremely slow. It is made even more
difficult by the increasing pressure of population growth. The
capacity to save is much less, of course, where the population

expands more rapidly than the national income, so that real income per capita decreases. The rate of saving will be low because of the relatively small amount of real income in excess of that needed for subsistence. The process of accumulation is further retarded by the fact that institutional saving in these countries is in its embryonic stage, and the use of money as a medium of exchange is limited.

The number of persons at a level above that of bare existence in these populations is so small that it defies any attempt to squeeze from it savings for capital formation and subsequent investment. Where consumption levels are distressingly low, political and social forces make a policy of forced savings as good as useless. Theoretically, such a policy could be put into effect by heavy taxation, extremely low wages, and the introduction of what would almost amount to forced labor in village communities. Resistance to these measures, however, in any but rigorously totalitarian regimes would be so formidable as to defeat any such policy. It would be even more difficult to apply such measures because of the visible "demonstration effect" of Western civilization and its living standard, as well as the far-reaching effects such a policy would have on international political relations.

Thus it might be said that rapid capital formation in such countries is possible only through coercion and that a totalitarian regime would be the one most efficient and effective in applying such coercion. Under a democratic system, moreover, with the economy run on the basis of a multiplicity of private decisions made by factory owners, other employers of labor, landlords, and the like, there can be no certainty, and perhaps little probability, of diverting to investment the resources created by depressing living standards and decreasing consumption.

There is no guarantee whatsoever that capital, if it becomes available, will be used for investment and the promotion of economic growth. In some of the underdeveloped countries a small but wealthy minority at the top of the ladder has considerable resources in its hands and squanders most of them in conspicuous consumption. Further, a considerable proportion of this accumulated capital is being exported to the developed nations of the world; this is particularly marked in the Middle East, where there are immense incomes from oil royalties, and in Latin America. The England of the Industrial Revolution used its accumulated resources for investment in order to expand its production capacity, but this does not mean that the same course of action will be followed in Saudi Arabia. The will to apply resources properly, with knowledge, skill, and entrepreneurial initiative, is the indispensable prerequisite to economic growth.

This, of course, does not mean that savings, even forced savings through taxation, are precluded from playing any role in the economic growth of those underdeveloped nations operating within a democratic framework. The importance of savings would grow after the initial push and take-off in economic growth. A policy of providing for some lag in the upward trend of the standard of living as the gross national product rises rapidly—such as incentives for voluntary savings and tax relief—could have the effect of accelerating the process of capital formation for large-scale investment. Nevertheless, the "great leap" in nontotalitarian countries could be effected only by supplementing with outside assistance the capital formation based on savings. Such assistance could be a substitute for the methods of early capitalism and for those of today's totalitarian regimes as well.

IMPORT OF CAPITAL

A striking instance of what can be achieved by capital import as a substitute, in part at least, for the primary formation of capital is provided by the settlement and development work in Israel. Of course, the fact that a very rapid economic development was achieved under a democratic and stable regime can be explained by several factors, of which the import of capital is only one, although a significant one. The particular political conditions, the spiritual background, the quality of human material, the tension in which the tremendous effort was rooted, the security conditions—all created a set of unique circumstances.

Import of capital did not, of course, do away with the need for certain policies that were bound to be unpopular. For a period a regime of austerity was imposed. Heavy taxation and the diversion of resources from consumption to investment were enforced. However, the financing of Israel's development on such a scale by means of internal capital formation, even if it had been possible, would have resulted in intolerable stresses and strains on the social and political structure of the country.

The result of the Israeli venture is all the more conclusive because it was carried into effect under the most difficult conditions. To begin with, the rate of demographic growth far exceeded that of underdeveloped countries. Israel's total population within seventeen years went up about 225 per cent, to more than three times what it had been when the state was founded. Second, the geopolitical and military background was adverse to development. Boycott and blockade became a serious handicap, and heavy expenditures for security were required. Third, part of the population had been accustomed to a European standard of living, and serious efforts were made to preserve that standard. Fourth, the framework of a poor and relatively underdeveloped country with scarce natural resources increased the difficulties of the task. Fifth, the occupational structure and cultural background of one section of the population was not adapted to the exigencies and needs of the new state. An occupational reshuffling of most of the population became imperative. Sixth, and finally, people coming from seventy different countries, who for the most part spoke the language of the country of their origin, were in some instances centuries apart in their development. This conglomerate community had to be welded into one cultural and national entity.

In spite of these difficulties a sustained growth was achieved, which is reflected in the annual average increase of the gross national product, in real terms, of about 11 per cent—from IL. 1,148 million in 1950 to IL. 4,965 million in 1964 at constant 1955 prices—and, within this same period, an increase in exports of goods from $30 million to $607 million in 1963 and $649 million in 1964. While in 1949 only 14 per cent of imports were covered by income from exports, by 1964 this figure had risen to 55 per cent. In 1949 the population of one million was supplied domestically with up to 50 per cent of their foodstuffs; in 1963, when the population had reached two and a half million, domestic production provided some 85 per cent of needs, at an incomparably higher standard of nutrition.

In his article in *Foreign Affairs,* Professor Galbraith sums up this development as follows:

> One country that has shown great advance since the war, including great capacity to make effective use of aid, has been Israel. It is singularly unendowed with natural resources. It has no oil wells, few minerals, insufficient water and not much space. But all of the four elements mentioned—high literacy and a highly educated élite, the sense and the reality of social justice, an effective government and a strong sense of purpose—are all present. So there is rapid progress. The Israelis, were they forced to it, would better do without their aid than without their education, their sense of shared responsibility and shared gain, their public administration and their clear view of their destiny.[2]

What has been accomplished in Israel proves that sustained economic growth at an accelerated pace can be achieved under a democratic regime. Substantial imports of capital, which permit a slower pace of capital formation, are an essential precondition of such development. Even if the *imponderabilia* which play such an important role in Israel are taken into account, this venture seems to allow for some universal conclusions as to the possibility of rapid and sustained economic growth within a framework of democracy and political stability, provided that a large import of capital over a sufficiently long period of time is maintained. A similar process took place in Taiwan, thanks to the generous economic assistance extended by the United States and the import of capital.

The Marshall Plan, or European Recovery Program, as it was officially called, provides on an immense scale convincing evidence that import of capital in large quantities and within a relatively short period of time is likely to produce the desired breakthrough. By increasing productivity and its consequences, Marshall aid did an enormous task of postwar reconstruction in devastated countries and by such means did a great deal to restore international equilibrium.

The significance of Marshall aid lies first and foremost in its having been a new departure, heralding subsequent developments of a similar nature: "For the first time in history, resources from one continent were to be channelled, deliberately and on a huge scale, into rebuilding production, trade, and stability in another."[3] In this sense, Marshall aid was the precursor of the organized assistance to underdeveloped nations of a later period.

It is true that in one respect the analogy between the Marshall Plan and similar undertakings in underdeveloped countries would be erroneous. The European countries are endowed with skill, know-how, an industrial tradition, and managerial experience to an incomparably greater extent than are the underdeveloped countries. However, the Marshall Plan had to encounter certain formidable difficulties. It was carried into effect during a period of physical shortages. The pent-up demands of the European countries, as well as inflated purchasing power, exerted irresistible pressures. At the same time the only country which was able to offer assistance on a substantial scale, assume responsibility for the plan, and mobilize its resources for the goals set, the United States, had not yet worked off the excess liquidity of its own economy. Domestic demand in the United States itself, four years after the end of World War II, was still subjecting its economy to stresses and strains. Moreover, the whole world had yet to overcome the many difficulties of reconversion from a war to a peace economy and of gearing production to the needs of peace.

Also, political opposition to the Marshall Plan as a unilateral transfer of capital from one continent to another was pronounced and vocal. The criticism was directed against a system of what were defined as "handouts"—which were, in fact, the very essence of the plan.

Over $13 billion was spent in the Marshall Plan. The total aid to other countries in the years 1947, 1948, and 1949 represented from 2.1 to 2.5 per cent of the gross national product of the United States per annum. In those crucial years during which the Marshall Plan was carried into effect, large amounts of capital poured into Europe, and the results were certainly encouraging. Within two and a half years, production in almost all of western Europe exceeded the prewar level. The pace of growth was much faster than that of the United States itself. Aid was extended mainly in the form of grants, while the counterpart funds were either applied to the reduction of the public debt, as a deflationary measure, or to increasing the productivity of agriculture and industry. It is worthy of mention that the original plan envisaged an expenditure of $17 billion, but the task of reconstruction was fully implemented with an expenditure of the sum of $13.6 billion.

Within one decade the dollar shortage, which had wrought such havoc in international trade, had been overcome. The reconstruction of Europe had been completed. Physical short-ages had disappeared, and the standard of living had risen. As a result, Europe today is in a position to contribute substantially to the assistance of underdeveloped nations, in spite of the fact that large amounts of resources are absorbed by defense needs.

The full success of the Marshall Plan operation is due, among other factors, to its huge scope, to its completion within a short period, and to its realistic approach to the problem of indebtedness. The point of departure was that, under the circumstances, assistance, if it were to achieve the main purpose of quick reconstruction, could not be based on extension of commercial credits alone. The rapidity, the gigantic scope, and the noncommercial character of the operation possibly saved democracy in Europe. At the same time, the difference between the task of the Marshall Plan and that of promoting the rapid development of underdeveloped nations must not be overlooked. The Marshall Plan envisaged a limited period of foreign assistance for the reconstruction of highly developed countries devastated by war. The underdeveloped nations have an average income below subsistence level, and the raising of these low standards to anything approaching tolerable levels must inevitably be a lengthy process.

In any event, experience shows that the way out of the vicious circle of demographic growth, limited capital formation, and pressure on limited resources lies in a breakthrough to be effected by a tremendous initial outlay of capital. This outlay could put into motion self-perpetuating forces of economic expansion and growth and by such means could bring about higher standards and new concepts of life, which in turn would slow down the pace of demographic growth.

Even the increase in food production is closely connected with the supply of capital:

> Another probable precondition for a yield takeoff would be capital—capital that was not required when the food supply could be expanded by simply bringing new land under cultivation. The capital required to purchase yield-raising inputs is not generally available when incomes are still at subsistence levels. Some 24 countries ranking as major producers of rice, wheat, or corn have average per capita incomes below $200 per year. Per-acre yields increased in 14 of these countries between 1935–39 and 1960–62; in 8 countries they declined, and in 2 countries they remained the same. . . .
>
> To describe the preconditions for a yield takeoff is, in fact, to describe the whole process of modernization and economic

development. The close association between the level of economic development and the capacity to raise per acre yields is clearly demonstrated in the grain yield trends of the seven geographic regions during the period from 1934–38 to 1960. Some regions raised yields dramatically. Others raised yields very little. North America, the most advanced region, raised yields 109% while Asia, the least advanced region, raised yields only 7%.[4]

The operation must be on a scale commensurate with the magnitude of the task. Import of a trickle of capital into the less developed areas remains a Sisyphean effort, always submerged and defeated by the growth of population and the declining standard of living. The introduction of capital and skill would have the effect of laying the foundation for an autonomous formation of capital after a period of initial growth, which could gather momentum and become self-perpetuating in the course of time.

The Capital Market. But the problem of large-scale capital transfer must be viewed, above all, from the angle of the capital market in countries able to export capital. The world-wide shortage of capital is becoming one of the most decisive and influential factors in the economic structure of the world. The demand for capital has been accentuated by powerful new economic, technical, political, and sociological developments in this postwar "age of dislocation and experiment."

First, let us take the second Industrial Revolution. Automation, or the replacement of labor by machines, the electronics industry, spreading out into hitherto unknown areas as an auxiliary branch of armament and as supplier of the new demands of communications, the use of atomic energy for industrial purposes —all of these require immense capital investment. They deeply affect general economic conditions because of the competitive advantage possessed by enterprises with a high component of fixed capital. This advantage compels other enterprises to accelerate their pace of re-equipment in order to reach a competitive level. Thus, the new Industrial Revolution produces two results: quicker obsolescence and a more urgent need for re-equipment of whole industries, and a higher ratio of fixed capital per unit of production. Re-equipment is being accelerated. The volume of capital to be used for this purpose in the United States alone in 1964 was estimated at $39 billion.

Second, there is the matter of rearmament. The immense needs of rearmament coincide with the new Industrial Revolution and create an additional claim on existing resources. Moreover, the developments in this field parallel those of industry in general. Less manpower and more fixed assets (long-range aircraft, ballistic missiles, etc.) are called for; vast quantities of capital equipment are needed, while the number of people under arms is progressively declining.

Third, there is the rising curve of world population. In the past sixty-five years the world's population has doubled, reaching the figure of 3.2 billion by 1964, and is expected to redouble in the next forty years. This stupendous growth generates new demands for housing, schools, roads, and, last but not least, capital equipment for the integration of the population into the machinery of production. It attracts capital to new investment made profitable through the expansion of a diversified domestic market. Contrary to all expectations, population growth in developed countries has not been arrested, but rather accelerated, and serves to stimulate demand and to galvanize dormant factors of production. The rise in the living and consumption standards of the developed nations accentuates this trend and contributes considerably to the expansion of domestic markets.

On the supply side, the flow of capital to investment is being diminished by the redistribution of national income. This reduces incomes in the higher brackets, a large part of which were accumulated and invested, and raises incomes in the middle and low ranges. The result is not only the elimination of social extremes but also an increase in aggregate consumption because of the rising living standards of those sections of the population which have a higher propensity to consume. Under conditions of full employment this rise in living standards decreases the share of income saved, accumulated, and invested, and increases the share of income consumed.

Thus, the rate of accumulation is decreasing through social progress, as a smaller share of income is saved and accumulated. This social transformation has invalidated the nineteenth-century prognosis of social polarization. Today, the economic and social gap between the worker and the employer in a developed country is much less pronounced than that between the worker in a developed country and in an underdeveloped one.

The supply of capital is also reduced by the bargaining power of trade unions, which affects the internal supply of capital in highly developed countries and has an even more powerful impact on the export of capital to underdeveloped countries. Thus there is a conflict of social and economic interests between the trade union movement in the developed nations and the vast populations of underdeveloped areas. It results in a diminished rate of savings and capital accumulation; higher consumption, with a larger internal market and greater and more varied and attractive possibilities of investment, in developed countries; accentuation of discrepancies between the prices of primary commodities produced by underdeveloped countries and the prices of manufactured products in the highly industrialized nations; and a rise in the price of capital equipment needed for the development of underdeveloped nations.

Of course, this clash of interests is not conscious and deliberate. The workers in the developed lands are among the ardent supporters of aid to underdeveloped countries. The rather indirect influence exerted on export of capital by rising living standards and the increased consumption made possible by rising wage levels is too complicated a phenomenon to be understood by many people, concerned as they are with their own individual problems. So far as the great mass of people is concerned, the esoteric character of intricate economic processes and the many ramifications and indirect effects of socioeconomic measures are unknown or ignored. It is impossible to gauge what the attitude of the labor movement would be if the contradiction between ideology and vested interests were raised to the level of political consciousness and action.

Another consideration is involved in the balance of payments problem. Rising costs, among which wages are one of the most important single items, frequently cause a decline of exports. So far, there is no evidence that rising costs have priced American exports out of the world market to any extent. But concern with the balance of payments problem in the United States after a substantial loss of reserves strengthened the opposition to extension of large-scale assistance to foreign countries. Any further deterioration in the balance of payments may lead to cuts in the massive transfer of capital to underdeveloped nations.

In this context, there is a degree of potential interaction between costs of production, including wages, and competitive ability, exports, the balance of payments, and large-scale transfers of capital to underdeveloped nations. The volume of capital available for export and investment in underdeveloped countries is being reduced by the very social progress and success of the trade unions in the highly developed nations.

To sum up, the demand for capital is increasing in developed nations because of the second Industrial Revolution, which triggered off a flow of new investment in industries with a high fixed capital component. Other causes are the demand for armaments; the rapid increase of population side by side with the rise in the standard of living, and inflation, which on the one hand reduces incentives for saving and on the other, contributes to the expansion of domestic markets.

In the period in which all these factors—re-equipment of industry, expenditure on armaments, and need for investment because of population growth—were operative, markets in developed countries also expanded, thanks to the general rise in the standard of living. Full employment, which is the fundamental principle of economic policy in all developed countries, increases the bargaining power of trade unions, secures rising incomes for the workers, and stimulates consumption. Demand is increasing again, markets are expanding, and a new need is arising to expand capacity of production by investment in order to supply the new and diversified needs generated by a rising standard of living.

The expectation of an easy capital market after a period of reconstruction following World War II has not materialized. A chain of technological discoveries and a booming home market in the mature economies of the West have claimed a growing share of capital for investment. This leaves only a small surplus for export to underdeveloped countries. At present, heavy investment demand presses with increasing force on the available supply of savings. The claim of developed countries on existing resources for new investment is expected to increase.

The theoretical assumption that the surplus of capital in the Western economies will be attracted to countries with underdeveloped resources because of higher potential returns, resulting from their supply of cheap labor and unexploited sources of raw materials, has not come true. Insecurity of the capital invested is only one of the factors working against extensive exports of capital to underdeveloped countries. The low productivity of the labor force, as well as its lack of skills, likewise discourages foreign investment. An expanding and diversified market, coupled with increasing demand, exerts a pull on capital to invest in already industrialized countries. The existence of auxiliary industries, of scientific institutions, and of all kinds of technical facilities is an additional stimulant to such investment. Capital is reluctant to break virgin ground in unexplored and underdeveloped areas so long as the lure of profitable investment in developed countries remains great.

Another attraction of the developed and industrialized countries is their money and capital market, with ample credit facilities on the one hand, and, on the other, the high liquidity of investment in shares wherever the stock exchange serves as an efficient instrument for shifting from liquid to fixed and from fixed to liquid assets. With a relatively high rate of profit in developed and industrialized nations, the natural flow of private capital is not channeled into underdeveloped countries, but rather in the opposite direction. Except for the capital that goes to those countries to exploit their oil resources, little is flowing according to the natural processes of economic gravitation.

The fundamental idea that surpluses of private capital should flow from highly industrialized to underdeveloped countries to be invested there is certainly very attractive, and, under conditions which prevailed for a long time, it is desirable and sound. Actually, however, the export of private capital from developed to underdeveloped nations stagnated during the years 1956 to 1961 at a rate of $2.5 billion per year, while the export of public capital during the same period doubled, going from $3 to $6 billion. Therefore, it is difficult to escape the conclusion that under conditions of a world shortage of capital plus investment demand in industrialized countries, a reappraisal of the prospects of such a development may become imperative.

> 1. The flow of long-term capital and official donations from the developed market economies to the developing countries and multilateral agencies, after falling back for two years, recovered much of the lost ground in 1964. . . . Altogether the flow of resources in 1964 (net of all repayments) reached a total just short of $8 billion, about 6 per cent above the previous year's figure but not yet back to the 1961 peak.
>
> 2. During the period 1961 to 1964, production in the developed market economies continued to expand vigorously. As a result the ratio of resource transfers to the developing countries to gross output in the capital-exporting countries declined to below 0.7 per cent in 1963 and 1964.[5]

But only a large inflow of capital could augment the productive capacity of underdeveloped nations. It would also slow down the pace of demographic growth: the connection between a rising standard of living and reduced demographic expansion is manifest.

The point has been made that, in some countries, the level of cultural and technological development and the training of manpower are more important than the provision of capital, and that there is also a category of countries in which the first precondition of economic growth is social reconstruction and reform. It should, however, be borne in mind that to raise cultural and technological levels by vocational training and other means necessitates, primarily, a substantial amount of capital. A technological and vocational lag does not mean that the countries so retarded can dispense with the transfer of large resources to them: it means only that the major part of the capital investment must be made in human resources and the rest in material goods. Second, the countries in which a shortage of capital is the main impediment to development have populations larger than those in the two other categories. Third, even under present conditions, George D. Woods, the president of the World Bank, could report to the Development Assistance Committee that "a preliminary Bank inquiry based, for each country, on the judgment of the Bank's country specialists and area economists, suggests that between now and 1970 the less developed countries might productively use an additional $3–4 billion a year."[6] At present, the supply of capital is woefully inadequate. It is a far cry from an annual $3 to $4 billion of additional funds recommended by the Bank.

The Burden of Debt. But apart from the insufficient flow of capital, which is ascribable to a reluctance to invest in underdeveloped countries that is well justified by economic conditions, a serious question arises as to the extent to which underdeveloped nations are able to meet their debt service obligations on huge monetary commitments based on commercial rates of interest and periods of repayment which are normal and reasonable for private capital. The heavy burden of debt is aggravating an already ominous situation. The terms on which assistance is given are such as to bring about, in the long run, an equilibrium between aid and repayment of loans, principal and interest. The Organization for Economic Co-operation and Development has summarized accumulated data on debt servicing as follows:

> Public and publicly guaranteed external debt of 37 less-developed countries, covering roughly three-quarters of the population of the (non-Sino-Soviet) less-developed world, increased from $7.0 billion at the end of 1955 to $21.5 billion at the end of 1963. The annual average rate of increase was about 15 per cent. Partial information available for a number of important less-developed countries suggests a continued rapid increase in 1964. It is hardly necessary to say that wide variations exist among the records of individual countries.
>
> Service liabilities (interest plus amortization) on the same categories of debt for the same 37 countries increased still more rapidly from $0.7 billion in 1956 to about $2.7 billion in 1964. In spite of the progress which has been made over the years in providing loans on soft terms from official sources, these debt service liabilities increased for 1959–1963 by about 17 per cent per year, and the latest estimates indicate a further increase of 14 per cent in 1964. It is estimated that about two-thirds of total debt service payments in any one year on official and officially guaranteed loans are accounted for by guaranteed private export credits, mostly short-term. Many of these credits are replaced by other credits in the normal course of foreign trade. In most less-developed countries external debt service liabilities have increased at a considerably higher percentage rate than exports of goods and services, gross national product, or savings.[7]

It is estimated that the problem will be even more vexing in the future, as 20 to 50 per cent of the external debts of the developing countries fall due in the next five years.

In an article in *Foreign Affairs* for January, 1966, Mr. Woods painted a frightening picture of what is going to happen if present trends continue:

> These levels of debt service are dangerously high. They mean that a good part of the countries' foreign-exchange resources

must be devoted to servicing previous obligations rather than to new productive development. Indeed, when all amortization, interest and dividend payments are taken into account, the backflow of some $6 billion from the developing countries offsets about half the gross capital inflow which these countries receive. These payments are continuing to rise at an accelerating rate, and in a little more than 15 years, on present form, would offset the inflow completely. In short, to go on doing what the capital-exporting countries are now doing will, in the not too long run, amount to doing nothing at all.[8]

In a speech on September 27, 1965, to the Boards of Governors, Mr. Woods again emphasized the gravity of the situation and the absence of any progress (and there is considerable evidence to corroborate his view):

At the present time, terms [of assistance] are not easing fast enough. Although the need for more favorable terms is universally accepted in principle, and the United Kingdom and Canada have recently taken substantial steps in this direction, the improvement, on the average, has been small. Given the financial facts of life in the underdeveloped countries, a general easing of terms is clearly indicated if we are to avoid disaster in the future. Otherwise, cases of default and serious interruption of capital flow would seem to be inevitable. And harm done by defaults, in my opinion, is much deeper and more serious than the financial figures show; it is truly beyond calculation.[9]

The Agency for International Development of the United States Department of State published a report in 1965 reviewing the accumulation of international indebtedness:

The external debt of the developing nations is rising rapidly. For example,
— their total debt increased from $10 billion at the end of 1955 to over $30 billion at the end of 1964;
— annual debt service charges have risen from less than $1 billion in 1955 to well over $4 billion in 1964; and
— in 1955 external debt amounted to 7 per cent of the Gross National Product of the developing countries whereas it is now more than 15 per cent.
The capacity of the developing countries as a group to service

additional external debt on hard terms is rapidly diminishing. Several countries are already carrying such a heavy load of debt relative to their foreign exchange earnings that the World Bank, the Export-Import Bank and private lenders are reluctant to extend more credits to them.

There is much more at stake here, however, than the question of whether particular developing countries are considered credit-worthy by those who lend on hard terms. These countries must receive a continuing *net flow* of foreign exchange if external assistance is to contribute to their economic growth.

The extent of the net flow realized by a developing country from its foreign borrowings depends directly upon the amount required to service its foreign debt. If $100 is lent to country X in 1965, for example, and X has to pay out $10 on its foreign debt, the net flow of resources (i.e., the amount remaining in X's hands for development) is $90. If, on the other hand, X has to pay out $60 for debt service, the net flow is $40.

In the last 10 years, the debt service burden has increased so rapidly that it has cancelled out much of the growth in total aid. In 1955, 8 per cent of external assistance received was offset by debt service. In 1964 debt service offset 30% of external assistance. The effect of this is plain: whereas 92 per cent of the foreign aid provided in 1955 was available for development, only 70 per cent of the aid provided in 1964 was available for such use.[10]

The former president of the World Bank, Eugene R. Black, rightly calls attention to the fact that the borrowing countries are nearing the limits of their capacity to incur debts on conventional loan terms, and that

> in many countries too great a proportion of development aid has taken the form of debt, which has to be repaid in foreign exchange, and, secondly that of that debt, too great a proportion is short- and-medium-term debt, mainly of the supplier credit variety, the service of which places a heavy burden on export earnings during the next few years.

The report goes on to say that indeed

> in some countries the achievement of a reasonable degree of economic progress requires external development assistance on

a scale far surpassing any realistic expectation of the recipient country's capacity to repay on conventional loan terms. If development assistance is given on terms which are too burdensome, it will overload and eventually break down the structure of international indebtedness, with grave consequences for sound development financing.[11]

This problem is of particular importance in connection with investment in social overhead capital, such as railways, ports, and roads, which form the infrastructure of a modern economy and are indispensable for a process of industrialization and for the upsurge of primitive economies. The development of basic facilities, such as power, communications, and irrigation, is imperative as a precondition for attracting capital to secondary industries.

These facts have found increasing recognition and recently led to the establishment of the International Development Association, as a subsidiary to the World Bank. IDA's policy deviates in two important details from what has hitherto been considered the only appropriate method of assistance to underdeveloped nations. Long-term credit on strictly commercial terms is being extended for profitable and productive enterprises by the World Bank, and money is being lent on easier terms for projects connected with the social structure of a modern economy, such as housing, education, etc., by IDA.

Thus we are confronted with the problem of whether export of public or semi-public capital, state-to-state bilateral assistance, and multilateral international aid can be confined to the role of a spark to ignite private capital, which should follow suit but which so far has failed to do so. Paul G. Hoffman, in his pamphlet, *One Hundred Countries and One and One Quarter Billion People*,[12] estimates that the highly developed Western world would have to export $3 billion per year for the next ten years, over and above the present level of assistance, to raise the standard of living in underdeveloped countries by 2 per cent per person per year. His plan would cover about one hundred countries, and there is a general consensus that his estimate is a realistic indication of the order of magnitude of the task.

The World Bank committee for the study of development problems of India and Pakistan emphasizes that, between them, these two countries reflect the most important characteristics of the developing world. The committee rightly stresses that "perhaps the most striking feature of the sub-continent's development problem is its sheer scale: not only are real incomes low, but, with a population of about 500 million—about 90 million in Pakistan and over 400 million in India—the capital resources required to generate even modest increases in real income are very large."[13]

However,

> despite the many differences and contrasts between India and Pakistan, the basic economic problem confronting them is the shortage of capital resources in relation to the needs of development. In both countries there is the familiar vicious circle of low income, low savings, and continuing low income, which cannot be broken effectively without an inflow of capital funds from abroad. Both countries are suffering from a serious shortage of foreign exchange, and have been forced to impose strict import licensing.[14]

The committee states that their increase in resources, based on an increase in the rate of both public and private saving ranging from 8 to 12 per cent, is, in itself, a remarkable feat, but "both Ministers and officials recognise that the political pressures existing in a democratic society, which has only recently gained independence, impose a definite limit on the sacrifices of immediate consumption to the needs of the future which the government can ask of its people."[15] Underlying the committee's conclusions is their acceptance of the view that aid must consist for the most part of grants and loans and that it should not be confined to loans on strictly commercial terms.

The reconstruction of Europe after World War II was accomplished through a large-scale, ambitious plan of assistance, predominantly in the form of grants. The economic aid given to underdeveloped nations, in contrast, contains a large element of commercial loans and medium-term credit. It has already been pointed out here that the condition of these nations is hardly comparable with that of Europe after the war. Although devastated by the ravages of war, Europe preserved most of its infrastructure, including its skills, technology, and managerial experience and ability. The underdeveloped nations have had to start from scratch. Their ability to repay commercial loans on the scale now envisaged is at least doubtful. The question arises of whether the forms of economic aid utilized in the Marshall Plan would not now be appropriate for the underdeveloped nations, while the present methods of financing those nations might not be more satisfactory for the developed countries. Repayment of debts by Europe would now be very useful; it would certainly be possible; and it would alleviate the problem of international liquidity and the balance of payments problem of the United States. On the other hand, the financing of the development of poorer nations should be shaped on the pattern of the Marshall Plan.

A higher rate of internal capital formation could hardly be achieved under a democratic regime, and if the totalitarian solution is rejected, the assistance from abroad cannot be confined to a business transaction but must be extended by bodies which assume world-wide economic responsibility and shape their policies on a global scale. This concept is not new. The World Bank has pioneered in this direction and has paved the road for an imaginative approach to the solution of the problem. If the Western world has every reason to be gravely concerned about the growing disequilibrium between its own development and the progress of underdeveloped countries, it must concentrate its efforts in three areas:

1. assistance to underdeveloped countries in order to restore the desired equilibrium in their balance of payments by developing their resources;

2. maintenance of reasonable standards of living in these countries, and their gradual upgrading through the use of capital and skill;

3. elimination of tensions caused by violent economic fluctuations or precipitate declines in standards of living, which result from economic stagnation and deterioration of terms of trade.

It seems that in underdeveloped countries private capital, although indispensable in the long run, needs to be preceded and supplemented in the initial period by direct grants and substantial public loan capital of the kind now supplied by international agencies such as the World Bank, the IDA, and, on a bilateral basis, by the highly developed industrial nations. It has been argued that capital cannot be transferred artificially, but we have seen artificial equilibria established and maintained for the benefit of humanity. The so-called "built-in stabilizers" in developed countries, which have shortened and mitigated recessions and prevented economic crises, are, in a way, artificial. Nevertheless, they are today the accepted system of the entire Western world.

The underdeveloped countries cannot get directly, on the capital market and on the scale which is necessary, the capital required. They are unable to compete with developed countries in the free capital market, and they need financial intermediaries. No dogmatic adherence to "natural" capital movements should be allowed to mislead the world or influence the efforts of the nations who are trying to raise the standard of living and reduce grave and growing discrepancies.

A solution that relies upon an automatic flow of capital, self-propelled and driven by the quest for profits, does not meet the exigencies of such a situation. A completely laissez-faire solution could possibly work but would have to be all-inclusive and would have to include, in addition to a free flow of capital, a free interchange of goods and free movement of populations by migration. All three combined might eventually provide a solution based on the price mechanism. But the movement of goods is still hampered by all kinds of physical restrictions, such as bilateral trade agreements, currency controls, and customs barriers. There is certainly no freedom of movement for populations. Thus, under existing circumstances, such a solution is unrealistic. The flow of capital cannot be the sole exception to the general trend of a world economy beset with so many restrictions and distortions.

Rapid economic growth requires large amounts of capital if it is to become self-sustained and continuous. Isolated, fragmentary development is costly and protracted. Thus, a simultaneous approach to financing of the infrastructure—of education as well as of agricultural and industrial enterprises—in the short run may be more expensive but in the long run is much cheaper and more effective. The task is to extend the scope of this transfer of capital so that it will be commensurate with the urgent needs of the underdeveloped nations. Moreover, such capital transfer must be implemented on terms and conditions under which a projection of repayment becomes realistic.

Much has been done in this field by the World Bank and its International Development Association, but the relationship between the challenge and the performance is not satisfactory. The World Bank can lend only on commercial terms, and its loans are hard loans, as the funds of the World Bank are raised on commercial terms. Many of the developing nations cannot provide the collateral for hard loans and are unable to borrow because the terms are too onerous for them. IDA lends on terms well adapted to the capacity of those developing nations which are able to assume financial obligations for their economic development, but the means at its disposal are extremely limited.

The developing nations are already overburdened with debts incurred on commercial terms, and they can hardly meet the requirements of servicing such debts. The dilemma is obvious: the terms of the World Bank are too difficult, and the means of IDA are too limited. The flow of private capital does not increase and, according to the OECD figures already quoted (see p. 52), actually stagnated in the period 1956 to 1961, during which time the flow of public capital doubled. This flow of public capital is an encouraging development, which nobody would have dared to predict in 1956.

However, the crucial problem is that of the terms under which the flow of capital is arranged. The report of the Agency for International Development cited above (p. 55) throws some light on that problem:

> *The Relation Between Loan Terms and the Amounts of Aid Required for Development*
> The mounting external debt burden of the developing countries emphasizes the need for soft loan terms. Furthermore, if development loans are made on soft terms rather than hard, the job of development will be finished sooner and the United States and other donors will have to furnish less total aid.
>
> This follows from the fact that, as loan terms harden, the net flow of resources decreases. And a decrease in the net flow of resources has two effects: it lengthens the time necessary to do a given job of development, and increases the amount of aid required to do that job.[16]

Further, AID adumbrates four categories of loans:

1. IDA (the International Development Association, the affiliate of the World Bank which makes loans on soft terms): .75 per cent interest, fifty years maturity, including a ten-year grace period.

2. AID Minimum: 2.5 per cent interest, forty years maturity, including a ten-year grace period with 1 per cent interest.

3. AID Medium: 3.5 per cent, twenty years maturity, including a three-year grace period.

4. Hard (these terms are generally in line with those extended by the World Bank, the Export-Import Bank, and others; some international lending takes place on even harder terms): 5.5 per cent interest, thirteen years maturity, including a three-year grace period.

The conclusion from the analysis of these four possibilities is that "the net flow will vary substantially depending upon the loan terms that are used. The harder the terms, the less the net flow," and that "the cost of trying to achieve development on hard terms is clearly excessive—if, indeed, it can be achieved at all."[17]

To sum up, large-scale financing of investment on easy terms in developing nations seems to be the only way to prevent frustration and to narrow the gap between the developed and the developing parts of the world. Without new ideas and new methods the vicious circle of underdevelopment and poverty cannot be broken. Under the Marshall Plan, 80 per cent of the total aid given consisted of straightforward grants, and only 20 per cent represented credits. That was the policy toward countries with tremendous resources in human skill, investment experience, and managerial initiative. In developing nations which are devoid of these resources, most of the transfer of capital is on commercial or semi-commercial terms. Without a change in this pattern, there can be no massive transfer of capital to developing nations. What those nations need are grants or low-interest loans for long periods and on a tremendous scale.

CHAPTER 4

ECONOMIC EQUILIBRIUM

INFLATIONARY SAVINGS

In their search for new capital, the developing countries frequently turn to inflationary methods. In their attempts to finance development, they often strive to achieve forced savings by deficit financing of government budgets, a method which provides certain resources for investment. The delusion that resources for development can be appropriated by governments through inflationary savings is frequently aroused by the consideration that if a country refrains from ambitious development ventures, it *ipso facto* chooses stagnation, dependence on foreign assistance for its balance of payments, and an unacceptably low standard of living.

If monetary expansion takes place in a country with underutilized resources, expansion of the physical volume of production following upon monetary expansion through governmental deficit financing may galvanize dormant factors of production, which help to balance and set off the effects of monetary expansion. Here, to a great extent, the problem will be one of the pattern of economic expansion and selectivity of investments. Bottlenecks in the flow of skilled labor, raw materials, or equipment may frequently limit and retard the expansion of the gross national product, even though, on the whole, there are ample underutilized resources.

Selectivity of investment and deliberate adjustment of its pattern may release unused resources and other factors of production, by such means helping to overcome bottlenecks. Reorientation of investment may have one or more of several useful effects. It may bring about an increase in the supply of scarce resources, either by encouraging technical training or by introducing some specific equipment. It can also result in the elimination of projects that call for excessive quantities of a resource which is scarce. These are some of the means of overcoming bottlenecks, which, with monetary expansion proceeding, can cause serious inflationary pressures and all the economic distortions that such pressures bring with them.

The determination of the optimal relationship between investment in the infrastructure and in branches of the economy, which, after the fruition of the investment, will influence directly the balance of payments, either through replacement of imports or expansion of exports, is an important decision. Thus, from the point of view of controlling inflation, the utilization of capital imports is, in the last resort, no less important than their availability.

If resources are scarce, there is one decisive criterion for investment: to what alternative use can the resources be put? Too frequently, development projects in developing nations are judged and evaluated without proper regard for the order of priority. In the main, the question is seen as one of whether a certain project is desirable on its own merits, but seldom as one of whether an alternative use of the same resources for another purpose would rank higher in the scale of priorities. Selectivity as a guiding principle applies, of course, not only to capital but to total resources, including managerial and technical skills, which in many cases may be the main bottlenecks.

However, selectivity must also be used, on occasion, in considering the painful question of whether to refrain altogether from some less than urgent projects. Where total projects exceed available resources and the implementation of marginal schemes may subject the economy to stresses and strains leading to inflation, great selectivity is necessary. In the long run, inflation slows up development because of the difficulties of balance of payments, the physical shortages resulting therefrom, and the fact that prices rise so high that the money supply cannot be increased further in order to allocate resources to development.

Nevertheless, in a country of dormant factors of production and underutilized resources, the policy of monetary expansion may, under certain conditions, have the effect of galvanizing and utilizing otherwise idle production capacity, but only in the short run and to a limited extent. In countries in which, because of the already rapid growth rate or because of scarcities, there are no remaining dormant factors of production, or where the bottlenecks are of such a rigid character that they cannot be overcome by change in the pattern of investment, the situation is incomparably more complicated. If, in such countries, the monetary authorities validate, through an increased supply of money, claims exceeding in volume the sum total of resources, the fat is in the fire and inflation will take its course. In these cases the supply of money is being augmented either by government budgetary deficits and borrowing from the central bank or by excessive expansion of credit through the banking system. In the long run, inflation affects nearly every social group. In the short run, however, pressure to initiate an inflationary policy by such validation of claims and by excessive monetary expansion is a frequent occurrence. Almost every social and economic group becomes aware of the fact that in the short run it can gain by acquisition of assets through inflation, if it can succeed in maintaining its monopoly or supremacy in the appropriation of resources. This situation results both in rising price levels and in increased pressure on the balance of payments. The surplus purchasing power spills over into excessive demand for foreign currency to buy imported goods, a demand which cannot be met by increased production. This leads to a deterioration of the balance of payments. Depletion of foreign currency reserves, physical shortages, and unemployment caused by shortages of raw materials and other components of production that depend upon imports are the inevitable results of such a policy.

As alternative economic policies, development through inflation or economic growth within the framework of stability must, first and foremost, be subjected to the test of economic efficacy. Economic stability is not a value superior to all other values and is imperative only because it is a prerequisite for long-term sustained growth free of economic distortions.

Monetary expansion may be the result either of direct government deficit financing or of overextension of banking credit to private enterprises. Less frequently, it is caused by persistent surpluses in the balance of payments. In the latter case, the surplus of foreign currency is accumulated by its "monetization" in the form of local currency, which it creates and which exerts an inflationary pressure. This latter form of inflation is a rather rare occurrence in developing countries, where, with the continuous decline in the prices of primary products and the limited import of capital from abroad, balance of payments difficulties are usually encountered. Inflation generated by a surplus in the balance of payments is therefore a very rare exception.

In inflationary countries with a plentiful labor supply and a shortage of capital, equipment imported at artificially low rates of exchange replaces labor. Simultaneously with the pressure for more imports caused by the gap between the artificial and the real rate of exchange, exports are adversely affected by the disparity between the high level of internal costs, determined by inflationary pressures, and prices in international markets. This disparity is reflected in unrealistic exchange rates, which actually diminish the returns of exporters. The high level of the cost of production cannot be reflected in prices on the foreign markets because of international competition, while the equivalent of the foreign exchange earned is converted into local currency for the exporter at an artificially low rate of exchange. At the same time, because of the discrepancy between inflated purchasing power and the limited quantity of goods and services available, the internal market is ready to absorb the additional quantity of goods at high prices and can do so with greater ease than can be done in foreign markets. Productivity is reduced by the fact that the marginal utility of additional amounts of depreciating cash is usually low, which has the effect of raising leisure in the individual's scale of values.

A shift from essential to nonessential production will take place because the imposition of price controls, which usually occurs in such situations, primarily affects essential goods, keeping their prices relatively low. Free-floating purchasing power and income, however, become diverted to the purchase of luxury goods, which are uncontrolled and form practically the only outlet for inflated incomes. In these instances, the import of capital in the form of a transfer of currency becomes insignificant because the artificial rate of exchange, which overvalues local currency, is tantamount to an expropriation of a part of the capital imported.

Nevertheless, developing countries face a strong temptation to finance development by inflationary methods. By monetary expansion they try to overcome the handicap of low rates of saving and capital formation, and of inadequate capital imports from mature economies. The decline of savings under inflation, owing to the continuous depreciation of money, retards a capital formation which, in any event, must be modest. For a short time, monetary expansion creates a kind of artificial inflationary saving, and the government is able, by devaluation of money, to appropriate a large part of the national income and in this way to increase investment. The attempt to supplement, by creation of new money, capital equipment bought through supplier credit leads inevitably to deficit financing by government or to overexpansion of commercial banking credits, both of which are self-defeating expedients.

Attempts to control inflation under conditions of rapid growth encounter major difficulties. The overheated economic activity brought about by such conditions, together with overemployment and pressure on limited resources, becomes, as a rule, contagious and creates a vicious circle of new enterprises and new demands on resources. Moreover, the psychological effect of such conditions is normally the overestimation of resources and sharp competition for those available, with a consequent steep increase in the cost of the various factors of production. In such a situation, the emergence of bottlenecks becomes inevitable. This development is aggravated by an inclination toward spectacular investment projects. So far as young and developing countries are concerned, shortage of capital in these circumstances is mitigated only to a very small extent by capital imports.

In developing countries anti-inflationary policies encounter great difficulties, mainly because the success of the monetary policy applied by the central bank is to a great extent dependent on co-ordination with fiscal policy. Large budgetary deficits cannot be neutralized by the monetary policy of the central bank alone. The central bank usually has to execute its monetary policy under the pressure of monetary expansion caused by budgetary deficits. Central banks in developing countries are almost invariably subject to governmental interference, even if they have a certain formal autonomy. If budgetary deficits cause the money supply to expand, the only remedy is a tight money policy and credit restrictions. The orthodox means of influencing money markets, such as open market operations or the manipulation of interest rates, are not very effective in developing countries. An open market policy presupposes the existence of a money market, which in such countries is either nonexistent or very limited.

Resale of credits becomes a characteristic of these conditions. The crude system of obtaining money at nominal rates from banks and then reselling it at exorbitant rates in the private money market is one variation. The use of bank credit, at preferential rates of interest, in enterprises for production of goods is more frequent, the inflationary gain coming through the sale of these products on the free market at prices carrying the very high rate of interest of the free money market.

Under these conditions, credit policy is of the greatest importance. In developing countries changes in the cost of credit have relatively little impact on monetary expansion and contraction. The orthodox methods of control—manipulation of the rediscount rate and of interest rates in general—are of little importance, for the following reasons: (a) interest rates to meet the exigencies of the situation would have to be so high as to become politically and socially impractical; (b) the availability of credit is more important than its cost; and (c) the deduction of interest for tax purposes tends to blunt the effectiveness of this weapon.

Central banks, therefore, have to resort to quantitative and qualitative credit controls, liquidity ratios, and similar devices in order to keep the quantity of money in check. High liquidity ratios imposed on commercial banks may prevent further inflationary increases of bank credit. However, the effectiveness of such a policy will depend on the measure of quantitative expansion of central bank credit to government. The central bank can apply its policy of monetary contraction and credit restriction only within certain limits. If these limits are exceeded, large-scale unemployment may result, compelling the central bank to reverse the process.

The limitations on quantitative controls because of political and other external pressures do not warrant the conclusion that monetary policy is entirely ineffective in curbing inflationary pressure and neutralizing the detrimental effects of monetary expansion. It is probably the most effective available means for the partial sterilization of an excessive quantity of money, which was generated in the first place in an attempt to overcome the shortage of real resources, such as internal savings and influx of capital. The full effectiveness of monetary policy will depend upon its co-ordination with budgetary and fiscal policy and upon the elimination of the fundamental factors which generate inflationary pressures.

For developing countries which do not possess dormant factors of production or unused resources that can be galvanized by monetary expansion, an inflationary solution is self-frustrating. Dormant factors of production must include not only manpower and equipment but also an optimum combination of labor, raw materials, and equipment if they are to be effective in a development plan. Monetary expansion which exceeds the capacity of production (calculated on the basis of the optimum combination of all the available factors—skill, labor, capital, and raw materials) will not increase the gross national product, even if there is a deficiency in only one factor. It will lead first, to depletion of foreign currency reserves and later, to physical shortages. As the opportunities to obtain (largely from abroad) additional means of production diminish, this artificial prosperity will also diminish, and the volume of money chasing scarce goods will have an immediate impact on prices, availability of goods, and the balance of payments.

Under conditions of limited capital import, slow capital formation, and the reluctance of the owners of what accumulated capital there is to invest it, the temptation to generate resources where none existed by means of budget deficits becomes almost irresistible. Monetary and fiscal discipline then breaks down completely. However, even under such conditions, there are instruments available to control inflation to some extent.

Savings, and even forced savings through taxation, can serve as an important source of noninflationary financing. The resources at the disposal of some segments of the population can be diverted to investment by a system of incentives and disincentives, as well as by taxation, and conspicuous consumption can be discouraged. As for taxation, heavy duties on commodities ranging from the nonessential to the semi-essential can serve as an important instrument for diverting resources from consumption, particularly from conspicuous consumption, to investment, thus making inflationary financing of development superfluous. The next step could be the development of a capital market capable of gradually absorbing some of the surplus accumulated by entrepreneurs, landlords, etc. The lag of income behind production and productivity could be provided for by a wage policy slowing up wage increases and diverting the resources thus made available to investment.

All these methods of promoting capital accumulation and saving and diverting surpluses to investment can only be successful if, during the transitional period, a too rapid increase in consumption is prevented, monetary discipline is maintained by the authorities, and monetary expansion is kept within the limits of the actual increase in production. Of course, this policy presupposes the existence of facilities for the kind of research that would prevent any overestimation of resources.

As to the institutional organization of the machinery for the control of inflation, its most important feature must be a central bank with broad powers and far-reaching autonomy. Such a bank is essential first and foremost as an instrument of credit control, because inflationary developments can originate from the commercial banking system just as easily as from government budget deficits. The central bank can also serve as a watchdog over the government, not only in preventing the use of the printing press to finance and accelerate development, but also in influencing the general attitude toward problems of inflation and combating any tendency toward creation of an inflationary gap. This is made more important by the fact that the psychological effect of overheated economic activity and boom is to encourage attempts to do too many things at once.

But even if all the brakes are applied, they may prove ineffective in the long run. They may slow down the process to the level of a creeping inflation, but even then the ability of the economy to compete on the world market is undermined. In such cases, an early readjustment of the rate of exchange serves as an indispensable and formidably effective means of restoring equilibrium. If such an operation is delayed, the result can be very costly in terms of resources and their utilization. This surgical method of controlling inflation is, of course, used only as a last resort.

The process of inflation itself will be greatly influenced by the size and pace of the import of capital. On the one hand, if the import of capital exceeds the excess of imports over exports and leads to the accumulation of foreign currency reserves, which are monetized, it can become in itself a vehicle for the promotion of inflation. On the other hand, ample import of capital from abroad counteracts the temptation to carry out development by internal monetary expansion.

The importance of political and social forces in applying the brakes of an anti-inflationary policy cannot be overemphasized. The temptation to accelerate development even under conditions of rapid growth is intensified by the very existence of a rapid rise in production and of boom conditions. As is well known, the policies of pressure groups are determined by short-run prospects, and all pressure groups are interested in inflationary developments.

Overestimation of resources is nearly always a concomitant of conditions of rapid growth. Governmental limitation of monetary expansion to the range of production growth as measured in real terms, credit control, and forced as well as voluntary savings are all unpalatable remedies from the point of view of the public. So is the lag of income increases behind production growth. Selectivity of investment in order to assure an economically rational pattern encounters great difficulties. Devaluation, the last resort of an anti-inflationary policy in a later and more pronounced stage of inflation, is politically inexpedient and, if only for reasons of prestige, always encounters opposition. In its attempt to apply the brakes in a situation of rapid economic growth, the central bank is usually exposed to pressure both from the government and from the public. Any action to control inflation under these conditions must, therefore, combine economic measures with an effort to educate political forces to a policy of sound growth within a stable framework.

EXPORT OF CAPITAL AND CAPITAL FORMATION

What is urgently needed is an international economic equilibrium, to be brought about by the direction of the flow of capital equipment to areas where it is most needed, and, simultaneously, the attainment of a high level of employment in the mature economies producing such equipment. If the deterioration of standards of living in the underdeveloped countries could be arrested by such means, this fact alone would shorten and mitigate the recessions that may occur in industrialized countries. Export of capital goods to the less developed parts of humanity would open up new avenues of production and employment.

The decline of purchasing power in the underdeveloped countries must have repercussions on the economic situation in mature economies and may aggravate conditions favorable to economic recession. In the underdeveloped countries, it causes difficulties in their balance of payments and retards their progress towards a higher standard of living. Export of capital can bring about fuller use of existing resources in highly developed countries. Increasing productivity and far-reaching mechanization, including automation, are already causing technological unemployment in some countries. In the developed world the diversion of resources to the production of commodities that supply artificially created needs has recently provoked much adverse comment: this diversion is taking place at a time when conditions in the underdeveloped world are desperate and when amelioration of such conditions should be of paramount interest.

Of course, the economic effect of an artificial expansion of internal purchasing power and the effect of a transfer of capital to the underdeveloped nations would be the same. The abolition of the "bogey of maturity" and the reduction in the margin of underemployed resources could be important by-products of large-scale investment in underdeveloped nations. Such investment could be made by allocating a certain proportion of the gross national product of the industrialized world for this purpose; for example, 1.5 per cent of the GNP of the developed nations would amount to about $15 billion. The existence of structural changes in mature economies should reinforce the interest of developed nations in such a plan.

The most pronounced swings and cyclical fluctuations occur in the production of capital equipment and of durable goods. They are the most vulnerable sectors of a modern economy and frequently are the sources of recessions or economic weakness. A balanced economic growth, therefore, depends upon a rising curve of production in heavy industry producing capital equipment. In the periods of economic recession in the United States after World War II, the decline was most pronounced in the durable goods sector. This observation seems to indicate that these sectors are the key to the prevention of cyclical crises and recessions. Experience has proved that in recessions the contraction of production of durable goods is, in most cases, four to five times larger than the contraction of the GNP.

It can be seen that in periods of economic recession in the United States following World War II the decline was most pronounced in the durable goods sector. Export of capital goods and equipment to underdeveloped countries would increase the scope of production in these branches and would bring about a decrease of cost per unit of output, thanks to economies of scale.

In the light of these facts, the export of capital to underdeveloped nations becomes doubly significant. The developed nations could considerably increase their production of capital equipment and durable goods, thus reducing unemployment in large sections of heavy industry. The problem would be one

of timing and of co-ordinating the export of capital equipment to underdeveloped nations with the cyclical declines in the
domestic market.

The prosperity of the last decade, which made America and
Europe so much wealthier, as well as the more even distribution
of wealth between them, has enabled the industrialized and
highly developed nations of the West to extend their assistance
to the underdeveloped nations on a greatly expanded scale. The
very elimination of Europe's deficit in its balance of payments
with America, the accumulation of foreign exchange reserves in
Europe and their depletion in America, imposed new obligations
on the nations of Europe, which were drawn into involvement in
practical action to promote the development of the underdeveloped nations.

Western Europe increased its production in the nineteen fifties
by some 5 per cent per year, in comparison with a little over 3
per cent per year in the United States. Europe is becoming a
major economic force in the world, comparable to the United
States and the Soviet Union, and is able to participate in the
tremendous task of developing other parts of the world.

In ten years Europe's dollar reserves increased by $15 billion.
Western continental Europe is now the largest market for the
primary producing countries: in 1962 it bought as much as 36 per
cent of their exports, while the United States accounted for 30
per cent and Britain, for 21 per cent. Moreover, the saying that
"if America sneezes Europe gets pneumonia" is no longer valid
since the remarkable revival of economic activity in Europe and
the increase in European gold balances. The postwar recessions
in the United States did not shake the foundations of the
European economy and did not hamper its economic activity
very seriously. It is becoming increasingly clear that the European economy is becoming to a large extent independent of
economic developments in the United States.

Europe, in which the OECD member countries (including
Turkey) had a population of about 350 million and a gross

national product of about $375 billion in 1963, has become a powerful economic and political body. The unification of six of its countries in a common market may greatly facilitate its division of labor and bring about more efficient utilization of resources. The creation in the heart of Europe of such a large and diversified market may well confer on the countries of the European Common Market the advantages of large-scale production. The advantages of optimal location of centers of production will be fully enjoyed. The rich resources of coal, iron, and power; the wealth and productive capacity of northern France, western Germany, the Benelux countries, and northern Italy; the accumulated capital, equipment, experience, technical skill, and managerial ability—all make the Common Market organization a new and formidable idea. Convertible currency and multilateral trade, high standards of science and technology, must further invigorate this industrial giant.

The Common Market area today is without doubt the wealthiest and most industrialized in Europe. It assumes the character of an economic bloc, and its power is rooted in a progressive division of labor and an accelerated capital formation, thanks to a rapid increase in production and large imports of capital. The McGraw-Hill Economic Institute, known for its forecasts of the distribution of capital, has analyzed American capital investment in foreign subsidiaries. A survey covering three-quarters of all such outlays by American firms reveals that in 1960 American investment by manufacturing companies in their foreign affiliates and subsidiaries was 21 per cent higher than in 1959.

It has been predicted that this trend will be intensified in coming years. In this way, American companies are able to circumvent customs barriers surrounding prosperous markets. The trend is particularly pronounced in the flow of capital to the countries of the Common Market. In 1960 these countries attracted 24 per cent of the total capital exported by American industrial companies to their subsidiaries abroad; in 1959, this figure was only 17 per cent.

The distribution of American capital investment abroad (in absolute figures) is as follows: to Common Market countries, $160 million in 1959, $270 million in 1960, and $360 million in 1961; to other European countries, $220 million in 1959, $230 million in 1960, and $290 million in 1961; to Canada, $220 million in 1959, $240 million in 1960, and $230 million in 1961; to Latin America, $170 million in 1959, $250 million in 1960, and $240 million in 1961; to other countries, $110 million in 1959, $130 million in 1960, and $180 million in 1961. The "other countries" are those of Asia and Africa, which comprise the bulk of the areas and nations which are defined as underdeveloped. The flow of capital to these countries is relatively small, both in scope and rate of increase.

Of course, the new-found unity of the Common Market is based not only on economics but also, to a great extent, on politics. A new political force in the richest, most industrialized part of Europe is emerging and is projecting itself into the world arena. This new shift of economic power and activity resembles the great shift from the Mediterranean to the Atlantic in the past, and from Europe to the United States in the period between the wars.

But the renascence of Europe means not only power but also new responsibilities. General de Gaulle has already stressed assistance to the underdeveloped nations as a central task of the community of developed and industrialized states and as an important safeguard of peace.

Concern with the balance of payments in the United States reinforces this new departure, which should bring in its wake a redistribution, between Europe and the United States, of the burden of financing the development of underdeveloped nations. Thus, in spite of the fact that the United States is confronted with a balance of payments problem, the potential sources of foreign aid are now so much more numerous that an increasing flow of public capital to the underdeveloped world has been possible. Europe is wrestling with many political problems, and its participation in the financing of development projects in needy countries is not only a responsibility but also a requirement of enlightened self-interest. The coincidence of the war in Vietnam with a campaign in the United States against poverty and with overheated economic activity in Europe may momentarily invalidate this analysis and these conclusions, but a long-term trend remains and will surely assert itself even more strongly in the aftermath of present developments.

CHAPTER 5

THE DECADE OF DISAPPOINTMENT

In a resolution adopted on December 19, 1961, the United Nations General Assembly proclaimed the nineteen sixties to be the "development decade." This roseate vision contrasts gloomily with what has in fact taken place. For the last fifteen years or so, agencies have been extending financial assistance to the developing nations, and considerable amounts of capital have poured into the underdeveloped world. Yet the results thus far have been disappointing, and the danger that development activity in the world may become a fool's errand is very real.

The president of the World Bank, in an article in *Foreign Affairs* for January, 1966, described the situation as follows: "Unless the Development Decade, as President Kennedy christened it, receives greater sustenance, it may, in fact, recede into history as a decade of disappointment. The amount of finance moving from the developed to the underdeveloped world is not rising; and the present trend is for the growth of the low-income countries slowly to lose momentum."[1]

We are, then, faced with the possibility that the development decade may become a decade of failure and frustration. If the gap is perpetuated, if standards of living in some countries remain more than thirty times higher than in others, if up to two-thirds of the world's population are still hungry, or underfed, or both, the result may be unrelieved calamity.

The success or failure of the development decade must be judged not by intentions but by performance. There is one conclusive test of progress in the underprivileged nations—the rise in the gross national product per person. This criterion is applied by the United Nations World Economic Survey, which states that the annual rate of growth was 4 per cent in 1964, a figure which represents a steady decline from the levels reached in the nineteen fifties. Countries whose increase in gross national product was less than 5 per cent per year accounted for 66 per cent of the gross national product of the developing nations in the nineteen fifties and for 69 per cent in the early sixties. In the last five years the less developed countries outside of Europe have increased their gross national product by about 4.5 per cent annually. Thus the average per capita annual increment was less than 2 per cent. If a longer period is considered, the evidence of the inadequacy of such growth rates is equally impressive. It is also worth mentioning that, as a rule, economic growth in its initial period is likely to be relatively rapid. It is much more difficult to achieve a swift rise in already developed countries, where the absolute volume of the gross national product equivalent to each per cent of growth is so much larger. The Economic and Social Council of the United Nations, at its sessions on July 30 and 31, 1965, adopted the following resolutions:

Noting that more recently the net flow from developed to developing countries has virtually ceased to increase, and given the substantial growth in the national income of developed countries, progress towards the 1 per cent goal for resources transfer to developing countries has halted,

Further noting that payment of interest and repayment [of] principal on account of international debts incurred by developing countries is seriously diminishing the net inflow of new resources from the developed countries into the developing countries,

Recognizing that payment of interest and repayment of principal on international loans incurred for development is adding to the payment difficulties of some developing countries and seriously affecting their capacity to promote economic and social advancement to the desired level, . . .

The Economic and Social Council,

Concerned that at the mid-point of the United Nations Development Decade the rate of international flow of long-term capital and aid continues to fall short of the target of 1 per cent of the national income of the developed countries set out in General Assembly resolution 1711 (XVI) of 19 December 1961 and recommendation A.IV.2 of the United Nations Conference on Trade and Development and that the servicing of external debt constitutes an increasing burden on the resources of the developing countries, . . .[2]

Recognizing that at the mid-point of the United Nations Development Decade the rate of growth of the national income of most developing countries has been considerably lower than the modest target of 5 per cent per annum; that the gap between the standards of living in the developed and developing countries has widened instead of narrowing; that agricultural output in most developing countries has been disappointing in the light of the objectives pursued, that the pace of diversification of the economies of the developing countries has been slow and therefore the goal of self-sustaining growth remains as distant as ever,

Recognizing further the slow growth of export earnings of the developing countries and their inadequacy to finance their development needs,

Regretting that the flow of international capital to developing countries through various channels has been growing at a rate much lower than that required to meet development needs and that the burden of servicing past inflow of capital is threatening to retard the pace of growth in many developing countries, . . .

Recognizing that the rapid growth in population in many developing countries in relation to the growth of their national income calls for the most urgent action,

Aware that the developments in science and technology have placed in the hands of mankind the means necessary for abolishing poverty, ignorance and disease, . . .

Requests the Secretary-General and the executive heads of the specialized agencies and the International Atomic Energy Agency to review their work programmes and to explore the possibility of formulating future programmes of action and, if possible, to make projections over the next five years with a view to identifying areas in which their organizations can make their maximum contribution both individually and by concerted action to the goals of the United Nations Development Decade, and to report thereon to the forty-first session of the Council.[3]

This evaluation of the progress of the development decade by so authoritative a body is certainly both conclusive and instructive. The only way out of the impasse is a breakthrough to economic development by, in the initial stage, a massive transfer of capital. Capital alone cannot, of course, effect the economic breakthrough to self-sustained growth, but import of capital is an indispensable prerequisite to any progress. Economic growth is, to a great extent, a function of investment. But investment through slow infiltration of capital is ineffective in the long run, and a frontal attack on a large scale is much cheaper and much more successful. The autonomous formation of capital in the amounts required by countries at or below the subsistence level would, however, be politically and socially (and sometimes also physically) impossible. The only alternative is a substantial transfer of capital from the developed world.

The Organization for Economic Co-operation and Development has recently published a summary of the net total official and private flow of capital to the less developed countries.[4] It amounted in 1961 to $9.2 billion; in 1962, $8.5 billion; in 1963, $8.5 billion; and in 1964, $8.7 billion. The total private long-term net flow dropped from $2.6 billion in 1961 to $1.9 billion in 1962 and to $1.9 billion in 1963, rising again to $2.4 billion in 1964. The multilateral contributions amounted in 1961 to $842 million; then contracted in 1962 to $664 million; in 1963, to $384 million; and in 1964, to $367 million.

But these figures, depicting a plateau, are crude and must be analyzed if we are to realize the rate of the deceleration of assistance to underdeveloped nations. First of all, the reduced amounts went to a population which grew in the period in question by some 8 per cent; second, prices rose very considerably and so diminished, in real terms, the assistance extended; and third, the gross national product of the developed nations went up in that period by some 15 per cent. In relative terms, therefore, the cut in assistance was more pronounced than the figures themselves would indicate. The effect of all three factors —the demographic expansion of developing nations; the rise in prices of commodities, mainly manufactured products from developed nations, with a simultaneous drop in prices of their own primary products; and the fact that the reduced amount of capital represents an even smaller proportion of the gross national product of the developed nations as that product increases—is cumulative. The developed nations have chosen an alternative means of maintaining their levels of employment and economic activity: they are trying to increase consumption and demand in already developed nations.

The developing nations depend for their progress on import of capital per capita of population; otherwise, economic growth cannot be promoted. Wherever such import of capital was adequate—in Israel, in Taiwan, and in Puerto Rico, for instance —economic growth was satisfactory.

There is no magic or miraculous way of achieving even the most modest goals and hitting the target of a higher standard of living. In the light of these figures and against the background of demographic expansion, price rises, and enlargement of the gross national product of the developed nations, economic assistance is, in relative terms, decreasing. The projection for the future is more alarming still. Even in food production the key factor is the availability of capital.

Of course, the failure of the development decade to reach its targets cannot be attributed exclusively to a shortage of capital. The effective utilization of resources and the massive transfer of capital are of paramount importance and are predicated in the developing countries on the existence of the following conditions:

1. prevention of capital flight;

2. a taxation system which would promote the formation of capital and would mitigate the grossly unequal distribution of wealth and income;

3. land reform directed toward the same objective and adapted to the technical needs of agricultural production;

4. selectivity of investment and balanced expansion of the infrastructure and industrial capacity of production;

5. a planning system which would subject investment to the test of alternative use of resources and would avoid ill-considered investments in spectacular projects;

6. proper and significant allocation of resources to education, economic planning, and acquisition of know-how;

7. extension of facilities for family planning; and

8. appropriate measures of monetary restraint and preclusion of all attempts to substitute inflationary savings or inflationary financing of development for genuine capital formation.

The application of appropriate measures and policies cannot be a precondition of the transfer of resources but should accompany and follow the flow of long-term capital. These policies, which could evolve gradually and are parallel to the process of growth, would have to concentrate on a three-pronged approach on the part of the developed nations—massive transfer of capital, introduction of unilateral free trade, and a conscious effort toward a new division of labor, which would shift traditional industries to the developing nations.

ECONOMIC POLICY

Development is a long-range operation based on the integration of various elements, such as capital transfer and capital formation, skills and know-how, managerial ability, demographic planning, and proper utilization of resources. First and foremost, capital import must be supplemented by capital formation in the developing countries themselves. The developing nations must contain inflationary pressure. It is imperative that they concentrate on useful economic schemes and avoid mere spectacular, prestige projects.

Another precondition for proper development would be demographic control; frequently, development is unable to catch up with the rapid increase in population. As a matter of fact, standards of living in some of the developing nations are declining in spite of rapid development. The most effective remedy for this frightening decline is the conscious determination of the demographic process itself, by means of family planning. The connection between demographic control and the objectives of development, which require an allocation of resources to family planning, is obvious.

Another important consideration is availability of skilled labor and organizational and managerial talent. In theory, the underdeveloped countries are capable of cutting short the path to higher standards of living by profiting by the experience of the highly developed, industrialized states. Recourse to the collective memory and experience of the developed parts of the world presupposes the existence of a technological elite that can draw on such experience. Therefore, technical and scientific assistance and the training of scientists, instructors, managers, technicians, and other experts is the key to the effective utilization of economic aid. President Kennedy's plan for the establishment of a Peace Corps recognized the fundamental fact that financial assistance is not enough in itself but carries with it the responsibility of providing large-scale technical assistance. Here again, a focusing of resources on the creation and acquisition of skills is imperative.

Important, also, are policies directed toward proper utilization of such resources as are available. The exploration of physical resources forms an integral part of the mass of information that must be available for economic and physical planning. All these priorities have to be met at the time when capital is brought into a country to establish an infrastructure of the economy and to implement individual industrial and agricultural projects.

Import of capital alone, then, is no panacea. In some of the developing nations themselves there are serious shortcomings and deficiencies of policy which jeopardize rapid economic growth. The recent report of the Bank for International Settlements shows a substantial export of capital from developing to industrialized nations, which in some of the developing nations offsets their total influx of capital. These, of course, are ominous statistics. What is the use of transferring capital to developing nations only to have it find its way back to its source? The end and purpose of the whole operation thus becomes invalidated.

Political slogans are not enough. What is needed is solid achievement. The developing nations must stop the flight of capital and establish a taxation system adequate to tap their own resources. They must contain inflationary pressures. And, as has been said, it is imperative that they concentrate on useful rather than spectacular economic projects. The inclination to give preference to large-scale projects and dramatic ventures frequently dissipates the effect of the capital imported into an underdeveloped country.

Another dilemma is the relation of fixed capital to labor. Many such problems are involved in establishing a scale of priorities, which, if frustration is to be avoided, must be based on qualitative as well as quantitative controls. Replacement of labor by expensive machinery in countries with a surplus of labor and a shortage of capital, as well as the addiction to dramatic projects, is the most frequent and striking shortcoming in the qualitative control of investment.

Scarcity of capital can be alleviated by the proper utilization of resources. As has been noted, the order of priority of investment is of the greatest importance. But the criterion for the order of priority cannot be solely that of commercial profit. The proper development of the infrastructure of the economy—education, health, transport, irrigation, power, housing—is an essential condition for self-sustaining growth. But haphazard and piecemeal action, dependent on budgetary allocations from year to year, cannot produce useful results in terms of economic growth. Active integration of all the relevant aspects of economic and social life in underdeveloped nations necessitates, therefore, a planned import of capital over a period of at least several years and a co-ordinated approach to economic, social, administrative, and demographic problems. Of course, even the greatest efforts have their limitations. The most efficient utilization of funds, the import of trained personnel, and the best possible organizational plan and order of priorities will all be of no avail if capital import is not sustained and augmented. Only a proper combination of all these factors can promote and accelerate development.

The economic breakthrough effected through import of capital in developing nations is, under present economic circumstances, the only alternative to a total collapse of democracy, with the subsequent sacrifice of the rights, comforts, and expectations of several generations for the sake of rapid development leading to self-sustained growth.

On the other hand, achievement of rapid economic growth also depends upon the economic policy of the developed nations, particularly their trade policy, i.e., on the access of the products of the developing nations to the markets of the industrialized world. International trade is of decisive importance for the economic growth of the developing nations. The actual condition of such trade today is very clear: there is a cumulative and persistent deficit in the trade of the developing nations with the industrialized nations. Traditional exports cannot keep pace with increased imports, with the result that efforts to accelerate development are defeated. Industrialization and diversification of the economy, which is the only practical solution for the developing nations, is precluded by such an imbalance, which makes a substantial formation of capital impossible and saps the economic strength of the developing nations.

As a counterweight to this form of deficit trading, from which the industrialized nations greatly benefit, such nations should extend their share of the facilities essential to the growth of exports from the developing nations. In the absence of limitless capital imports from the developed countries, ever-increasing import requirements can only be satisfied by rapidly expanding exports and, in particular, exports of manufactures and semi-manufactures. The pronounced dependence of such countries on foreign trade for production, employment, and their very economic existence makes them particularly susceptible to fluctuations in international trade and thus eligible for special consideration.

The trend toward regional integration in the developed countries makes access to their markets even more difficult, and thus the relation between industrialized and developing nations must be based on principles different from those which govern trade relations between developed nations. Such a claim on the part of the developing nations is fully justified, if only because the decline in the prices of primary products is of great benefit to the industrialized nations and is tantamount to a transfer of capital to them. The former Secretary-General of the United Nations, Dag Hammarskjold, declared in one of his speeches that if the prices of goods exported by the developing nations should decline by 5 per cent, all the economic assistance extended to them would be wiped out.

Access to the markets of the industrialized nations on a preferential basis would involve the elimination of customs duties and other barriers to trade from developing nations. Such free-trade facilities would have to be unilateral and could not be matched by reciprocal concessions on the part of developing nations, for, under the circumstances, some protection of their infant industries is imperative.

The underdeveloped countries, however low their levels of production, must be afforded at least the opportunity to export if their economic life is not to be ruined altogether. This is the essence of the idea behind unilateral free trade. Preferential treatment to developing nations would make their industrialization possible and would at the same time promote a new division of labor. The expansion of industries producing capital goods would in the long run amply compensate the industrialized nations for any possible contraction that might occur among certain of their traditional industries and would help to reduce the danger of recession, which is always a prospect in mature economies.

The deterioration of the terms of trade of the developing nations represents a structural long-term problem and calls for an early remedy. The fact that the industrialized nations benefit greatly from declining prices of primary commodities and the consequent need for compensatory financing for the developing nations is recognized in various degrees, from the present short-term arrangements of the International Monetary Fund to the plans of the International Development Association for more far-reaching activities.

From this limited beginning, the new approach could expand gradually to its full consummation, in the form of preferential treatment for the developing nations. Admittedly, this is a tall order and would require some readjustment in the economic pattern of the industrialized nations. Industries experiencing diminished trade as a result of this new policy would have to be helped to adjust themselves, and workers affected would also need some help in finding appropriate new employment. Preliminary investigations, however, bear out the truth of the contention that the dislocation caused by such an adjustment would be small indeed.

Such a forward-looking and generous attitude on the part of the developed nations need not involve too great a sacrifice on their part if the quantitative scope of the problem is considered. The World Economic Survey for 1962 shows that an increase in imports of manufactured goods from the developing countries, whose value is estimated to be $10 billion in 1980, would represent only about 1 per cent of the additional demand for these same goods. Moreover, the exports of manufactured goods of underdeveloped countries amount to about 5 per cent of their total imports of manufactured goods and only 1 to 2 per cent of their total production of manufactured goods. If the proposed extension in the form of preferential treatment were to be applied gradually, the scope of the problem would be narrowed even further.

The idea of nondiscrimination in trade is, in itself, most laudable. But there is no such thing as equality between the starving and the overfed. Such a notion of equality has long been recognized as antiquated and obsolete in the domestic sociology of all the developed nations, and the welfare state discriminates in favor of the economically weaker sections of the population; progressive taxation is, in itself, an example of such discrimination.

This principle is valid in trade as well as in other aspects of economic life, and it justifies preferential treatment of the weaker, developing nations. It does not contradict but, as a policy, could fulfill a progressive and simultaneous role alongside the Kennedy Round, and that, in itself, would help to mitigate some of the difficulties of world trade. In any event, the problem is so complicated and of such great importance to the economic life of the world that such an approach is fully justified and most desirable.

Free access for the manufactured products of the developing nations to world markets would accentuate the shift of the industrialized world to sophisticated growth industries, such as electronics, atomic energy, and chemicals, as well as capital goods. In the long run, such a departure would amply compensate the industrialized nations for any possible contraction of production in some light industries producing simple consumer goods. It would create new purchasers for the capital goods of the highly industrialized countries and so be of benefit to all. The shift from traditional to sophisticated industries in the developed

nations would be tantamount to a shift to higher-income industries. The new division of labor which is taking place anyway
should be promoted, not discouraged.

Economically, the only realistic solution of the problem of the
developing nations is the industrialization and diversification of
their economies. Commodity agreements, compensatory financing, and so on, are desirable palliatives, but the long-term
solution is to be found only in structural changes in their
economies, and it is evident that such changes can be brought
about only through an economic breakthrough prepared for by a
massive transfer of capital and investment.

Development is a function mainly of investment, although
other factors, such as skill, proper administration, and planning,
are also essential. These other factors themselves, however, to a
great extent depend on funds for training, education, and so on,
which are not available if capital transfer is inadequate. This is so
because the internal formation of capital in countries with an
extremely low standard of living must of necessity be a slow and
agonizing process. Admittedly, such massive transfers of capital
and investment on such a large scale involve some waste, but
that is the price of projecting the welfare state and a tolerable
level of human existence onto a global scale.

CHAPTER 6

A WORLD
WELFARE COMMUNITY

The rich, highly developed, and industrialized North has to face two clear alternatives—confrontation or integration with the poor, undeveloped South. The Congo, Vietnam, Laos, and Indonesia may become the harbingers and precursors of a world-wide confrontation. On the other hand, integration, to be effective, must be rapid, decisive, and comprehensive. What is being done now—a trickle of aid, which does not even assure the *status quo*, but only generates friction and bitterness—seems to represent the worst of both worlds. It leaves the "emerging nations" with a sense of having been wronged, and this, if it persists long enough, breeds aggressiveness.

Against the background of confrontation between the developed and emerging nations, all issues, both economic and political, tend to become distorted. Political stability and prosperity become, in this small world, more and more indivisible. To paraphrase Abraham Lincoln's famous saying, the world cannot remain half prosperous and half destitute. There is a functional connection between peace and prosperity.

For the underdeveloped nations, it is a race against time. The need for a solution of their problems is made more urgent by the demonstration effect of standards of Western society. Further, demography and development reflect two conflicting trends. While population growth increases the urgency of development,

it also makes such development more difficult, until the peoples
engaged in this race against time despair of breaking the vicious
circle by democratic means.

A combination of three factors—spectacular demographic
expansion, decline in prices of primary products, and inadequate
capital flow into underdeveloped nations—has changed the com-
plexion of the political, social, and economic problems of the
world. The *détente* between East and West is postponed, as the
underdeveloped nations, most of which are politically uncommitted in the struggle, provide a new and promising arena for
the world conflict.

There is increased demand for and diminishing supply of
development capital. It is available where resources are plentiful,
but there is little incentive to pour it into areas with scarce
resources, even where the full utilization and rapid development
of such resources is urgently needed. The low rate of saving and
capital accumulation in underdeveloped nations, resulting from
low national incomes, precludes these nations from raising their
own capital. Technology and social engineering, as well as the
application of the economic and social sciences and the limitation of population growth, can provide a solution to the problem
if based on a farsighted, imaginative policy on the part of the
highly industrialized nations of the world. Meanwhile, the
struggle for the good will of politically uncommitted and
economically underdeveloped nations is continuing unabated.

Demography and geography are formidable factors in the new
struggle for power as the danger of a world conflagration seems
to recede. The apocalyptic specter of a nuclear war, after which
there could be no victors or vanquished, becomes less and less "a
continuation of policies by other means," as war is defined by
Clausewitz; and the difference between the "means" in peace
and in war becomes a qualitative and abysmal difference
between being and annihilation. War is not contemplated as a
station on the road to a given set of political objectives but as a
terminus under the shadow of death. As survival in such a war

becomes less probable, the myth of a heroic contest is destroyed, and, instead, the instinct of self-preservation asserts itself to an ever-increasing degree. As the literal finality of this "last resort" sinks into the minds of nations, the struggle for power through ideological and other means gains in importance.

Geopolitically speaking, a redistribution of power is taking place. Numbers become important. It is not only the number of soldiers that counts. Demography and economic assistance, together with ideological penetration, determine the pattern of the geopolitical world structure. The Afro-Asian bloc, with negligible military resources both in conventional and in nuclear arms, is nevertheless a powerful political factor. The area extending from the Sudan to Japan comprises twenty-four national states. If we divide these states into three categories—democracies, semi-democracies, and dictatorships of the left or the right—we find that there are only five states in the first category and three in the second, while sixteen are dictatorships. In this entire area, inhabited by more than half of humanity, only two-tenths of one per cent of the population still lives under colonial rule. These are striking and relevant facts.

Several defeats were inflicted on democracy in the last decade, mainly because the gap between the ability to grasp the intricate problems at issue and to make clear-cut decisions is deepest and widest in those countries. So it came to pass that the spectacle of these shortcomings encouraged resort to totalitarian ideology as a short cut to the solution of the complicated economic and social problems of the modern state.

The correlation between high standards of living and the democratic welfare state in Europe and low standards of living and totalitarian regimes in Asia is not accidental. Poor economic conditions are not the only cause of totalitarianism, but certainly they are a very important one. Thus the fate of democracy in the underdeveloped world is, to a great extent, dependent on the scope and speed of economic development.

It has already been said that the memory of colonial domination is very much alive in the consciousness of underdeveloped nations. The close co-operation of the Western powers in the past with some autocratic regimes in colonial countries helps to identify the West with groups which are hated by the masses of the population. In many of the developed countries, class conflicts on a national scale have become relatively insignificant, thanks to welfare state conditions, built-in stabilizers, fiscal and monetary policies, and so forth. The economic conflicts nowadays are not national but regional. The economic gap between the developed and the underdeveloped nations is incomparably greater than any that exists between the social classes within the developed countries.

However, ideological concepts persist long after the economic basis for their existence disappears. Semantics and intellectual orthodoxy perpetuate them. This is true both of class conflicts in the highly developed welfare states and of the anticolonial reactions in the underdeveloped countries, where colonialism is remembered in its crude form of political domination and economic exploitation. The maintenance of democratic regimes in the free nations of Asia and Africa is, therefore, an essential objective of the international policies of the Western nations, which cannot view with equanimity the collapse of democracy brought about by the slow pace of development and low standards of living.

The problem is really one of scale—of making the effort commensurate with the magnitude of the emergency. The resources of the North are great enough to overcome, in the course of time, the discrepancy between the needs and scope of action in the South. What is needed is a leap, a breakthrough. The growth of the gross product of the world is so rapid, and its size is so huge, that an allocation of a relatively small part of it for development of underdeveloped nations could launch the latter on the road to self-sustained growth. Only 1.5 per cent of the annual gross national product of the industrialized nations would amount to some $15 billion per annum, an amount adequate to tackle the problem of tensions and differences between the various regions of the world effectively and within a relatively short period of time.

The mature nations, however, have become tired of extending aid to the developing nations by budgetary allocations. The total inflow of capital, public and private, has represented in recent years some 0.7 per cent of the gross national product of the industrialized world. This balance sheet of deceleration in assistance and investment is most discouraging. Moreover, as the repayments on debts increase, the situation will deteriorate further, and there is a danger that at some point we shall reach something very near an equilibrium between receipts of new assistance and repayment expenditures on old debts. Could there be a more severe indictment of the methods applied? The institutions engaged in promoting economic development may reach a peak of respectability, but it will also be a peak of futility.

On the other hand, capital is available on the free markets of the world on an immense scale. Over $30 billion worth of fixed interest debentures and bonds is issued per annum on the financial markets of the industrialized nations. The bridge between the developing nations and these capital markets cannot be erected by means of free competition of the developing with the highly industrialized nations on these markets. Such resources can be tapped for the developing nations only by a combination of intergovernmental aid and commercial transactions. Relatively small amounts of money provided by the rich nations of the world on a governmental and multilateral basis could act as an ignition spark to generate a vast transfer of capital. This multiplier effect could be achieved by a negligible allocation to an interest equalization fund, and by a guarantee by developed nations that would make possible the mobilization of private capital on the financial markets of the world for underdeveloped nations.

This is, on the face of it, a bold plan, and it is justifiable to ask whether the allocation of 1.5 per cent of the gross national product of the developed and industrialized countries for this purpose is realistic. There are two striking historical examples of the feasibility of such a measure. The first is that of World War II, when the minimum allocation of resources to the war effort was between 30 and 40 per cent, and in many cases exceeded that rate. Of course, this was a special case of temporary emergency, the feat being made possible by a rather drastic reduction in the standard of living, which would be impossible in peacetime. However, the difference between 1.5 and 30 to 40 per cent is so large, and the increase in the gross product of the developed world has been so immense, that the conclusion seems justified that an allocation of 1.5 per cent would not seriously affect the normal economic life of highly developed countries.

The second example is that of the Marshall Plan, which has already been referred to in some detail. It, too, absorbed about 1.5 per cent of the gross national product of the United States in a period during which there was strong pressure on existing factors of production to supply internal demand. This demand, pent up during the war period, had been made at a time when, in absolute amounts, the national income was much lower than it is now and when the diversion of a part of it was much more difficult. Nevertheless, the Marshall Plan did not impair the normal functioning of the American economy.

Moreover, the mere fact of full utilization of the capacity of production itself increases the total gross national product. It is well known that the steel industry, which could serve as a basis for production of capital equipment required by underdeveloped nations, is far from being fully employed in the United States. So long as there are dormant factors of production, the possibility of the allocation of a part of the gross national product for development purposes exists, with concurrent increases in the total gross national product because of fuller utilization of dormant factors of production and general stimulation of economic activity.

Of course, the problem is to a great extent one of the composition of the gross national product and its division between private and public consumption. Thus, the developed countries are confronted with the problem of the reorientation of their economy: instead of stimulating internal consumption by promoting waste, the surplus production obtained under conditions of full use of productive capacity and of the labor force would be earmarked for export of capital.

It would seem that export of capital instead of waste of resources, and a redistribution of consumption between the private and public sectors, would present a constructive solution of the problem. If it was possible to implement such a policy in the Marshall Plan, during a period of readjustment of the economy to peacetime needs and of excessive demand, and if it was possible to allocate at least 30 per cent or more of the gross national product to the war effort, it would certainly appear possible and desirable to allocate 1.5 per cent of the gross national product for a purpose which may well contribute to the prevention of war. An economy that is expanding and increasing its gross national product will yield to developed countries more than would be necessary under this scheme for export of capital and will create that permanent demand which stimulates production.

As to the formation of capital as a factor promoting economic growth, new information is provided by the OECD:

> One of the pertinent aspects of increasing the rate of growth is the process of capital formation. Whereas estimates on this item are less than satisfactory, some rough aggregate treatment may nonetheless be useful. On average, less-developed countries appear to have devoted somewhat more than 15 per cent of their GNP to capital formation during the recent past. In absolute terms this is estimated to be about $38 billion in 1963. On the other hand, the net flow of financial resources from D.A.C. Member countries to less-developed countries, both official and private and including amounts channelled through multilateral agencies, is estimated at about $8.3 billion for the same

year. If one assumes that most of this flow contributed in some way or another to capital formation in the less-developed countries, and one ought to make some allowance for relief contributions, one might conclude that D.A.C. Members made possible somewhat more than 20 per cent of the gross investment in the less-developed world as a whole.[1]

The disparity between the import of capital and the formation of capital does not, however, indicate that the import of capital is a negligible factor in promoting economic growth. It is important, even within its present modest compass, and, in the light of the balance of payments problems of developing countries, it is virtually indispensable, since it provides the foreign currency component in investment and development.

With a certain effort, an average rate of saving of some 15 per cent could be sustained in all those countries. With higher income, the rate would rise more than proportionately. On this basis, and assuming an allocation of 1.5 per cent of the gross national product of developed countries for the purpose, it should be possible, from the two sources—capital import and internal savings—to invest over $50 billion per annum in the underdeveloped countries. That amount would be greatly enlarged as gross national product goes up in the coming decade.

The 1.5 per cent allocation from the gross national product of the developed countries and the estimated annual savings of 15 per cent of the national income of the underdeveloped nations would be derived from sources that expand absolutely from year to year. When this fact is taken into account, it will be realized that the effect must be cumulative, producing a steadily swelling volume of capital available for investment in the underdeveloped parts of the world. If investment on such a scale is carried out rationally, it should considerably elevate the standards of living of the underdeveloped countries within a decade or so and thus narrow the gap between them and the developed nations.

However daring this aim may seem, there is no doubt that it can be served by capital inflow and investment, provided that these are selectively utilized and directed toward an early attainment of the stage of self-sustained growth. Economic growth along nontotalitarian lines must be made both feasible and attractive for the underdeveloped nations, particularly as they observe the growing influence of totalitarian solutions in Asia. On the other hand, the present situation cannot be frozen.

There are two formidable forces in the underdeveloped countries which lead to continued deterioration of standards of living. They have been referred to earlier but bear repeating. They are first, the demographic explosion, which, if unaccompanied by at least an equally large increase in output, seriously reduces the standard of living; and second, the decline in prices of primary commodities, which in some years has meant, for the underdeveloped nations, losses exceeding the sum total of the financial assistance extended to them. It is generally agreed that there is relative deterioration of the economic conditions of the developing nations, due to the demographic expansion and worsening of the terms of trade mentioned above, and to the crushing burden of payments of debts, both principal and interest, that were contracted on unrealistic terms.

The Managing Director of the International Monetary Fund, Mr. Pierre-Paul Schweitzer, in an address before the Economic and Social Council of the United Nations on February 24, 1966, vividly described what is happening today:

> Acute poverty has persisted in many countries, along with hunger and even the fear of famine. The gap between rich and poor countries remains painfully wide, with the advance of the poorer countries proceeding too slowly, and after suffering grievous setbacks.
>
> At the same time, there has been an unrivaled growth of world trade, a sustained and high level of economic activity in much of the world, and a solid strengthening of international monetary cooperation. . . . We are all acutely aware that hundreds of millions of the world's people still live under deplorable conditions. . . . We should, at the same time, recognize that an

adequate solution of the problems of the developing countries will not flow automatically from the growing affluence of a relatively few rich nations. This will require a sustained effort by all countries, over many decades.

The poor nations cannot save, and they cannot invest, and they must become poorer and poorer. It is a vicious circle and—to paraphrase Kipling—we shall reach the point where "North is North, and South is South, and never the twain shall meet." The rich will become wealthier, and the indigent will not be rescued from the abyss of destitution and despair.

On the other hand, as more such countries become independent, their political power is growing. Further, as nuclear war becomes more and more unlikely, the shape of things to come is being determined by political, social, and ideological pressures and counterpressures. This fact alone aggravates the sense of frustration which the peoples of the developing nations feel within the present economic pattern. Increasingly, they are shaping the face of the world to come. Half of the population of the world lives in Asia; the Afro-Asian and Latin American blocs are an increasingly powerful force in the United Nations, and they may be decisive in the great ideological and economic world contest. In a sense, by reason of their sheer numbers and geopolitical situation, these nations are being given something of the status of a great power in the international arena.

China is a striking example of the significance of population size. The growing weight of India in the council of nations is also a case in point. So is the political awakening of Africa. With the growth of international democracy resulting from the nuclear stalemate, and the shift in the struggle for power to the ideological and economic spheres, this trend is likely to be reinforced. The gap between the quality of the lives of the rich and of the poor peoples of the world, and between the political influence of the developing nations and their economic opportunities, creates an explosive situation.

The decisive question is whether this vicious circle can be broken. Is it only a paralysis of will that prevents the solution of the problem? Modern technology, to the miraculous progress of which tremendous achievements in space and on the surface of the earth bear such eloquent testimony, and modern economics properly applied are together adequate to solve the problem.

The agonizing fact is that the world must free itself from its prejudices and outdated dogmas and doctrines if the problem of development is to be solved, and progress in this direction has been small. How is it that the nations of the world cannot devote, at the least, 1 or 2 per cent of their gross national product to international development? The underutilization of physical and human resources in the developed world is estimated at $50 billion per annum. How is it that, in spite of this, only some $9 billion are available as aid for the most crucial and important task of this century? The United States alone was able to finance the reconstruction of Europe by means of the generous and formidable Marshall Plan, a few years after an exhausting war and at a time when it had to supply a pent-up demand in its own country. Now, the whole developed world is faced with the challenge of developing the underprivileged part of humanity at a time when the resources on both sides of the Atlantic are incomparably larger. How is it that what the United States could do alone cannot be done by the developed nations in unison? How is it that several major countries have been able to spend many billions on space exploration while the problem of development remains unsolved?

The gap is widening, and it is our duty to subject the story of this failure to a remorseless scrutiny. There are no insuperable obstacles, independent of human will, along the road to a better life for the whole world. This is not the first time that fallacies, prejudices, and financial ultra-orthodoxy have defeated a great and desirable project. We know now that the Irish famine of the eighteen forties could have been relieved without much difficulty if it had not been for a mistaken belief in rigid, unbending economic laws. We know that the great crises of the nineteen twenties and thirties in Europe, America and the whole developed world could have been averted by proper measures. This view is corroborated by the plain fact that no such economic crises have recurred since World War II. A comment of universal significance was made by Chester Bowles, United States Ambassador to India:

> One of the least happy facts of human evolution is that even the harshest economic experiences must be relived and the most costly lessons relearned. Consider, for instance, our own recent economic experience:
>
> Just thirty-three years ago fifteen million hungry, desperate, unemployed Americans were walking the streets in search of non-existent jobs, passing grocery stores overloaded with spoiling food for which there were few purchasers.
>
> For three long years this incredible situation had gradually been developing with no significant effort to correct or even understand it. As our economy stood on the brink of collapse, most privileged Americans were content to remark that although the spectacle was indeed distressing, we could be sure that sooner or later "natural forces" would again combine to restore a reasonable economic balance; in the meantime, the primary need was for public patience.
>
> By 1939 Franklin D. Roosevelt's New Deal had enabled us to expand our production, put several million people back to work, introduce a large measure of social and economic justice into American society, and establish a positive role for our federal government in economic affairs. Yet the most basic problem of all remained unsolved: in spite of our still massive unfulfilled human needs, one out of every six able-bodied men and women was unable to find a job.
>
> Faced with this paradox, some influential economists concluded that our economy had permanently lost its capacity for rapid expansion. From now on, they said, a substantial amount of unemployment would have to be tolerated, while we applied ourselves to the task of sharing more equitably the limited production that we had.
>
> Despite this widespread assumption of permanent economic scarcity, President Roosevelt called on the American people, shortly after Pearl Harbor, to produce five million tons of

shipping a year and fifty thousand planes. Many of our economists and virtually all our businessmen agreed that while this
might be a useful psychological gambit with which to worry the
Japanese and the Germans, as a practical matter it was reaching
for the moon.

But again the Cassandras proved wrong. Within two years we
went well beyond Mr. Roosevelt's targets to produce *twenty*
million tons of shipping and nearly *one hundred thousand*
planes. Moreover, at the height of the war effort in 1942, 1943
and 1944, we added to our massive military output more civilian
goods than in any previous year.

Thus under pressure of a world war Americans came to see
what we had failed to understand in peacetime: that there is no
earthly reason why unfulfilled human or capital needs should
exist side by side with idle manpower, idle tools, idle skills and
idle capital.[2]

One of the main reasons for the inability to deal with the
United States economic crisis of 1929 and with the world crisis of
the thirties was the exclusive concern with the financial façade
which concealed the real problem of material resources. However, since the later thirties, we have been aware that the
financial pattern must be seen from the point of view of material
resources and subjected to this supreme test. Without this
development in modern economic thinking, we would still be
deeply immersed in a world economic crisis, and the economic
stability of many nations affected by World War II would never
have been restored, as it was through the Marshall Plan. The
world should beware of becoming once again the prisoner of its
own prejudices. What is needed is an awareness of the urgency
of the problem and a new approach based on very simple
principles.

The first principle is that commodity agreements and compen-
sation assistance, desirable and laudable as such measures are,
cannot, in the long run, solve the problem of the underdeveloped
nations but can only alleviate it. The one way to narrow the gap
between the developed and the developing nations is to industri-
alize and diversify their economies.

Second, this objective can be attained only by transfer of capital on a scale which will encourage a breakthrough to self-sustained growth. Slow infiltration is futile. In the long run, a frontal attack on a large scale is much cheaper. Allowing for all differences between Europe and the emerging nations in skill, knowledge, and experience, the rehabilitation of Europe through the Marshall Plan in a short, concentrated period gave clear proof of what can be achieved by stimulating a breakthrough.

Third, it must be understood that the capacity of developing nations to absorb loans on commercial terms is limited. The conditions under which assistance is extended must be adapted to capacity to repay, if such assistance is to be of any use.

Fourth, the economic transformation of the world cannot be brought about on the basis of "business as usual." The efforts called for are, on the contrary, most unusual.

Fifth, some of the ideals of the welfare state, as applied internally among developed nations, must be projected into the global arena and made the guiding principle in relations between developing and industrialized nations.

If these guidelines are disregarded, all efforts to narrow the gap between the two worlds will be but a labor of Sisyphus. Past experience has made that clear. The problems with which we are concerned cannot be considered and understood without a sense of history. Two world leaders, President Johnson and President de Gaulle, have designated the gap between the rich hemisphere of the North and the destitute hemisphere of the South as the crucial problem of the twentieth century. The gross national product of the developed world today comes to $1,000 billion per annum, and it is expected to reach the astronomical total of $1,200 billion somewhere around the year 1970. A small proportion of this sum, reflected in physical resources—the only ones that count—transferred to the developing world could bring us much nearer to a solution of our paramount problem.

The situation bristles with contradictions and paradoxes. There is a trend toward decreasing assistance to developing nations at this very juncture. There is a grave risk that, instead of a freer capital flow to developing nations, we shall witness the reverse. And as the repayment of debts on onerous conditions goes on and the snowballing effect of interest payments becomes more marked, economic conditions in developing countries must inevitably worsen. Thus, economic rigidities produce their disastrous consequences.

It must be borne in mind that the main obstacles to the solution of these great problems are in the mental attitudes of people. Who would have dreamt in the twenties or thirties that Europe would experience an uninterrupted boom for twenty years, with a rapidly rising standard of living? Who would have guessed that the economic problem of the developed world in 1965 would be a shortage of labor? Economically, the twenties and the thirties in Europe and in America were an unmitigated disaster. There is much substance in the belief that, had it not been for that experience, World War II might have been averted.

How is it that profound economic crises were prevented after World War II, in spite of the fact that natural conditions and resources remained the same? What was eliminated? Had people become aware of economic fallacies, and had economics become to some extent humanized and subservient to great political and social aims?

In the developed parts of the world, the mechanics of modern economic life were finally recognized and were made subject to the will, objectives, and purposes of modern nations that had ceased to be prisoners of their own prejudices. The welfare state became the main achievement of democracy. We stand now on the threshold of a new era of international democracy, which may bring about the welfare community on a global scale.

There are two kinds of developed nations: one category suffers from an acute shortage of labor, and the other from underutilization of resources, together with unemployment. Both could derive substantial benefit from the diversion of resources to the tremendous task of promoting the economic growth of the developing nations. For those suffering from a shortage of labor and inflationary pressures, the manpower shortage and the overheated economy could be alleviated by giving free access to commodities from developing nations, promoting a new division of labor which would allow the latter to take over at least some of the simpler industries of the developed world.

Promoting the industrialization of developing nations, subcontracting the production of spare parts or ingredients of engineering industries, and the establishment of branches in other countries are the alternatives to importing labor on a scale that would involve the economic and social tensions that come with mass immigration. Moreover, as the income of the developing nations rises and their industrialization makes substantial progress, trade will be stimulated and a better balance will be achieved between the two worlds, promoting prosperity in both directions. Trade statistics show that while exports of the underdeveloped nations to industrial countries increased in the period 1955 to 1962 by 2.9 per cent (of which increase India, Hong Kong, Israel, and Mexico account for about half), during the same period trade between the developed nations expanded at a rate of 7 to 10 per cent.[3] The evidence seems to be conclusive that the development of underdeveloped nations would promote the exchange of goods and lead to prosperity.

There is, of course, the alternative of stimulating internal demand in those developed nations which suffer from underutilization of resources. The implication is an economic one. Export of capital goods to the less developed part of humanity may shorten and mitigate the periodic recessions in industrialized countries by opening up new avenues of production and employment. The full utilization of existing resources in highly developed countries would be greatly facilitated by export of capital.

The "bogey of maturity" looms in those highly developed parts of the world where there is a gradual widening of the margin between capacity of production and actual output. The alternatives are either stimulation of the export of capital to underdeveloped nations or increase of internal expenditure, mainly through governmental channels.

The President's Council of Economic Advisers, in a comprehensive study, "The American Economy in 1961: Problems and Policies,"[4] makes this estimate: "The gap between actual and potential output for 1960 as a whole can thus be estimated at 30–35 billion dollars, or 6 to 7 per cent of total output. . . ." The study adds: "Even the most prosperous nations cannot afford to waste resources on this scale." The estimate for 1961 is even higher: "This gap of about 50 billion dollars (1906 prices) defines the urgency of the economic problem facing the nation today and in the months ahead."

There is a close connection between this deficiency in production and the implementation of the plan to export capital to underdeveloped nations on the basis of an allocation of a certain proportion of the gross national product of the industrialized countries to that purpose. Moreover, the present situation in developed nations may worsen as defense expenditure grows less. Such expenditure has played a key role in stimulating economic activity in the highly industrialized nations. A prediction of a decline in defense expenditure is not based solely on the likelihood of general disarmament measures. With the so-called "overkill" capacity already in existence, armament expansion at its present pace ceases to make sense. It is well known that this problem is being thoroughly investigated by several governments and that a possible solution looms large on the political and economic horizon. There is, of course, the alternative possibility of stimulating internal demand in developed nations suffering from underutilization of resources by developing new needs and accelerated obsolescence; in fact, this policy is being carried into effect.

The question is one of priorities. A political and moral decision must be made as to whether or not economically and socially

artificial stimulation of internal demand, and accelerated obsolescence of equipment, should have priority over development of
the underdeveloped two-thirds of humanity in the South of the
globe. What is the present response to this question? It is
deceleration of the flow of capital, the whittling down of foreign
aid, and the erosion even of the idea of international assistance.
The total net amounts of capital available for the developing
nations may decline, even absolutely, through increases in
repayments, while the decline relative to the growing national
income in booming economies is already evident.

Access to free financial markets is imperative for the developing nations if the gap between challenge and performance is to
be bridged. This statement may appear to some extent hypothetical and unrealistic. However, the illusion of *Realpolitik,* which
brought in its wake the greatest economic depression of the
twentieth century and now perpetuates the plight of the developing nations, cannot serve as a guide in a modern world. At the
other end of the spectrum, an imaginative policy has brought in
its wake full employment, rising standards of living, economic
growth, the Marshall Plan, and the establishment of the World
Bank and the International Monetary Fund.

It should be borne in mind that the main obstacle to progress
towards self-sustained growth is not the objective condition of
the world, but rigid, antiquated, and obsolete economic thinking,
which is utterly unrealistic in the age of atoms and space.
Immediately after World War II, the spirit of liberation took
over from the miseries of war. However, the affluence of the
society of the sixties has caused a retreat from this spirit of
human solidarity. Economic saturation seems to weaken dedication to human values and objectives.

It is doubtful whether, in the atmosphere of today, the World
Bank could have been established. There would have been a
plethora of faulty arguments to prove that such an institution
was unrealistic and unnecessary. For that matter, the Marshall
Plan would never have been launched in an atmosphere similar

to ours, in which event Europe would have remained devastated, with disastrous results for the whole world.

Today, there is an inverse relationship between the possibility of effective action and the will to carry it into effect. The commitment to taboos and fetishes, the grasping at the shadow of money instead of the substance of economic processes, realities, and resources, are the great deficiencies of our time. They are the outcome of complacency. But there are also hopeful new departures in the world of ideas, in the intellectual search for a new way of thinking about these problems. Social conscience, political wisdom, and an understanding of the real interests of both industrialized and developing nations should establish a proper scale of priorities and give high preference to the development of two-thirds of humanity, even at the price of some slight slowing down in the expansion of domestic demand in the rich nations.

An imaginative approach to the great tasks of our century could play the same role that the countercyclical policy in the developed world did in eliminating economic crises in the postwar world. Such a policy would not only narrow the gap between the two halves of humanity, but would also make more prosperous those embarking on that great venture. As the rich North and the poor South face each other, one of the greatest dramas of human history unfolds. Nothing short of a global Magna Carta can save the world from a confrontation fraught with grievous dangers.

NOTES

Preface

1. U.S., Congress, Senate, *Foreign Aid—Message from the President,* 87th Cong., 1st Sess., 1961, House Doc. 117.

2. United Nations, Economic and Social Council, *Progress in United Nations Development Decade Evaluated* (Press Release EC|2278, June 2, 1965).

Chapter 1

1. Per Jacobsson, *International Monetary Problems, 1957–1963: Selected Speeches of Per Jacobsson* (Washington: International Monetary Fund, 1964), p. 182.

2. Escott Reid, *The Future of the World Bank* (Washington: International Bank for Reconstruction and Development, 1965), p. 61.

3. *Ibid.,* p. 63.

4. Lester R. Brown, "Population Growth, Food Needs and Production Problems," *World Population and Food Supplies, 1980,* American Society of Agronomy Special Publication No. 6 (Madison, Wis.: American Society of Agronomy, 1965), p. 3.

5. Lyndon B. Johnson, Special Message to Congress on the Food for Freedom Plan, reported in *Time Magazine,* February 18, 1966.

6. Reid, *The Future of the World Bank,* pp. 12–13.

7. Figures on developed countries are from *A Statistical Handbook of the North Atlantic Area* (New York, 1965). For developing countries, figures on gross investment are from *World Economic Survey* (United Nations, 1963). Figures on net investment are based on estimates by S. Kuznets, "Capital Formation Proportions, International Comparisons for Recent Years," *Economic Development and Cultural Change* (July, 1960). All investment figures are for 1960.

8. John H. Adler, *The Progress of Economic Development,* Talk before the Economics Roundtable Session of the Fifty-first National Foreign Trade Convention, New York City, November 18, 1964 (Washington: International Bank for Reconstruction and Development, n.d.), pp. 3–4.

9. *Ibid.,* pp. 8–11.

10. Eugene R. Black, "Address to the Economic and Social Council of the United Nations, New York, April 24, 1961" (mimeo.), p. 14.

11. Hermann J. Abs, Sir Oliver Franks, and Allan Sproul, *Bankers' Mission to India and Pakistan, February–March, 1960,* Letter to Eugene R. Black (Washington: International Bank for Reconstruction and Development, n.d.), p. 2.

12. Arnold Toynbee, *Population and Food Supply,* McDougall Memorial Lecture (Rome: United Nations Food and Agricultural Organization, 1959), pp. 15–16.

13. Raúl Prebisch, Secretary-General of UN Conference on Trade and Development, "Introduction," *International Monetary Issues and the Developing Countries: Report of the Group of Experts* (TD|B|32, TD|B|C.3|6, Nov. 1, 1965), p. 5.

14. *International Monetary Issues and the Developing Countries,* p. 7.

15. J. Marcus Fleming and Gertrud Lovasy, "Fund Policies and Procedures in relation to the Compensatory Financing of Commodity Fluctuations," *IMF Staff Papers,* Vol. VIII, November, 1960.

16. Jacobsson, *International Monetary Problems,* pp. 103–4.

17. Jacobsson, "The Economic Situation of the Western World," *Skandinaviska Banken,* Vol. XXXVII, No. 3 (July, 1956), p. 75.

18. *The Economist* (London), Vol. CCXVI (September 4, 1965), p. 892.

Chapter 2

1. Erich Walter Zimmerman, *World Resources and Industries* (New York: Harper, 1933), pp. 122–23.

2. Eugene Staley, *World Economy in Transition* (New York: Council on Foreign Relations, 1939), p. 73.

3. John Kenneth Galbraith, "A Positive Approach to Economic Aid," *Foreign Affairs,* Vol. XXXIX, No. 3 (April, 1961), p. 447.

4. Harold Butler, *Problems of Industry in the East, with Special Reference to India, French India, Ceylon, Malaya and the Netherlands Indies* ("International Labour Office Studies and Reports," Series B [Economic Conditions], No. 29; Geneva: International Labour Office, 1938), p. 73.

5. Royal Institute of International Affairs, *The Colonial Problem* (London: Oxford University Press, 1937), p. 275.

6. League of Nations, Economic Intelligence Service, *World Economic Survey: Eighth Year, 1938/39* (Geneva, 1939), p. 159.

Chapter 3

1. Chester Bowles, "Priority for Human Dignity," *International Development Review,* Vol. VII, No. 3 (September, 1965), p. 6.

2. Galbraith, "A Positive Approach to Economic Aid," p. 447.

3. Harry Bayard Price, *The Marshall Plan and Its Meaning* (Ithaca, N.Y.: Cornell University Press, 1955).

4. Brown, "Population Growth, Food Needs and Production Problems," pp. 13, 15.

5. United Nations, Economic and Social Council, *Financing of Economic Development: International Flow of Long-Term Capital and Official Donations, 1961–1964* (E|4079 Rev. 1|Add.1, Oct. 28, 1965).

6. *Statement of George D. Woods, President, World Bank Group, to the Ministerial Meeting, Development Assistance Committee, Organization for Economic Co-operation and Development, Paris, July 22, 1965* (Washington: International Bank for Reconstruction and Development, n.d.), p. 5.

7. Willard L. Thorp, *Development Assistance Efforts and Policies,* A Report by the Chairman of the Development Assistance Committee (Paris: Organization for Economic Co-operation and Development, 1965), p. 79.

8. George D. Woods, "The Development Decade in the Balance," *Foreign Affairs,* Vol. XLIV, No. 2 (January, 1966), pp. 211–12.

9. Woods, *Address to the Boards of Governors,* 1965 Annual Meetings, Washington, D.C., September 27, 1965 (Washington: International Bank for Reconstruction and Development, n.d.), pp. 8–9.

10. U.S., Department of State, Agency for International Development, *Summary Report of a Study on Loan Terms, Debt Burden, and Development* (Washington: U.S. Government Printing Office, 1965), pp. 4–5.

11. Black, "Some Principles for Development Assistance," Statement Delivered at a Meeting of the Development Assistance Group in Washington, D.C., March 9, 1960.

12. (Washington, D.C.: Committee for International Economic Growth, 1960).

13. Abs, Franks, and Sproul, *Bankers' Mission to India and Pakistan,* p. 2.

14. *Ibid.,* pp. 1–2.

15. *Ibid.,* pp. 13–14.

16. *Summary Report on Loan Terms,* p. 5.

17. *Ibid.,* p. 7.

Chapter 5

1. Woods, "The Development Decade in the Balance," p. 206.

2. United Nations, Economic and Social Council, *Official Records,* Suppl. No. 1, Resolution No. 1088 (XXXIX) (New York, 1965), pp. 7–8.

3. *Ibid.,* Resolution No. 1089 (XXXIX), pp. 8–9.

4. Organization for Economic Co-operation and Development, *The Flow of Financial Resources to Less-developed Countries, 1956–1963* (Paris: Organization for Economic Co-operation and Development, 1964), p. 20.

Chapter 6

1. Thorp, *Development Assistance Efforts and Policies,* p. 20.

2. Bowles, "Priority for Human Dignity," p. 7.

3. United Nations, Conference on Trade and Development, *Towards a New Trade Policy for Development,* Report by the Secretary-General of the United Nations Conference on Trade and Development (E|Conf.46|3, Feb. 12, 1964).

4. Council of Economic Advisers, "The American Economy in 1961: Problems and Policies," Statement before the Joint Economic Committee, Washington, D.C., March 6, 1961.

INDEX

Hemispheres North and South:
Economic Disparity among Nations

by
David Horowitz

designer: Edward King
typesetter: Kingsport Press, Inc.
typefaces: Caledonia
printer: Kingsport Press, Inc.
paper: Lidenmeyr Schlosser Book Smooth (clothed.)
        Lidenmeyr Schlosser Allied Offset (paper back edition)
binder: Kingsport Press, Inc.
cover material: